Florian Geiger

Mergers & Acquisitions in the Machinery Industry

GABLER RESEARCH

Schriften zum europäischen Management

Herausgegeben von
Roland Berger Strategy Consultants – Academic Network

Die Reihe wendet sich an Studenten sowie Praktiker und leistet wissenschaftliche Beiträge zur ökonomischen Forschung im europäischen Kontext.

Florian Geiger

Mergers & Acquisitions in the Machinery Industry

With a foreword by Prof. Dr. Dirk Schiereck

GABLER

RESEARCH

Bibliographic information published by the Deutsche Nationalbibliothek
The Deutsche Nationalbibliothek lists this publication in the Deutsche Nationalbibliografie; detailed bibliographic data are available in the Internet at http://dnb.d-nb.de.

Doctoral thesis, European Business School, Oestrich-Winkel, 2010

1st Edition 2010

Editorial Office: Ute Wrasmann | Sabine Schöller

Gabler Verlag is a brand of Springer Fachmedien.
Springer Fachmedien is part of Springer Science+Business Media.
www.gabler.de

Cover design: KünkelLopka Medienentwicklung, Heidelberg
Printed on acid-free paper
Printed in Germany

ISBN 978-3-8349-2293-9

Foreword

Which motives initiate managers to merge or to acquire other corporations? While there is a long-lasting history of empirical research on M&A in a cross-industry context, our knowledge about industry specific drivers of M&A is more than limited. Given this background, the machinery industry is an attractive segment to address questions on M&A motives – as it is on the one hand a very fragmented industry and on the other hand a bundle of in some parts highly consolidated sub-industries.

In his thesis, Mr. Geiger makes an effort to answer the question why firms in the machinery industry follow M&A strategies and how successful they are in their transactions. This is not only a remarkable endeavour because Mr. Geiger uses some hand selected unique datasets, but in particular, because he presents state-of-the-art analyses which are competitive and meet highest international standards.

The thesis on hand carefully identifies and addresses open research questions related to M&A strategies in a very specific industry. Its primary objective was to identify M&A motives for different types of companies in various sub-segments of the machinery industry by analyzing stock price and accounting data. Thusly objectifying managerial action allows deriving recommendations for financing practice.

Another focus of the thesis concerns the use of case study methodology to analyze the competitive advantages created by a merger in an already consolidated industry segment. The documented empirical evidence provides significant value added for the involved parties, in particular driven by transforming the competitive environment of producers in that segment into a competition with non price items as differentiating criteria.

Mr. Geiger fully achieves the objectives of this dissertation. The analysis contains many intriguing and surprising results which make this thesis an interesting read I highly recommend to corporate finance researchers and practitioners. I wish for a high, due circulation of this dissertation.

Professor Dr. Dirk Schiereck

Preface

Being involved in a number of merger transactions in the machinery industry in my function as a management consultant at Roland Berger Strategy Consultants my motivation for this thesis was to generate a broader understanding of the motives and influencing factors that initiate managers to engage in mergers or acquisitions and the drivers for success of such transactions. After extensive literature research I realized that the existing strand of theoretical and empirical research on mergers and acquisitions in a cross-industry context falls short to reflect the individual characteristics and specific drivers of the machinery industry. Consequently, I aim to fill this gap by providing extensive empirical research analyzing merger and acquisition strategies and motives of firms and evaluating their transaction success.

In my thesis, I follow a top-down approach focusing first on understanding underlying merger motives of managers in the machinery industry. I examine whether firms' merger motives are influenced by their prevailing industry environment. This strategic question seems especially important for machinery manufacturers as this industry is characterized by an heterogeneous compound of fragmented as well as concentrated sub markets. Based on a unique sample of 330 machinery transactions, I indirectly test for underlying merger motives applying statistical analyses on stock price and abnormal return developments. In a second step, I examine wealth mechanics and the success of merger transactions testing for various influencing factors presenting univariate and multivariate regression results. Lastly, to further cross the bridge from theory to practice, I apply case study analysis to enrich the empirical findings with practical lessons learned from one of the most successful merger and acquisition transactions within the last years. With my theoretical and empirical findings I am confident to provide practitioners as well as researchers insights into mergers and acquisitions that go beyond implications for the machinery industry.

This work would not have been possible without the organizational, theoretical, personal, and academic support from my doctoral advisor Prof. Dr. Dirk Schiereck. His critical questions, comments, and hints always helped to improve research and work quality. Also the discussions with my second advisor Prof. Dr. Andreas Wald enriched my thesis bringing additional aspects into analyses and interpretation of results. Special thanks also belongs to the Schuler AG, namely CFO Dr. Wolfgang Baur, who agreed in being interviewed for a detailed case study analysis providing numerous valuable information and interesting discussions. Thank you also to all other interview partners and friends who discussed methodology, research questions, and results interpretation with me. The variety of different perspectives helped to shape and round this dissertation.

Finally, I would like to thank my parents and family for their encouragement and advice. Thank you for always supporting me with all possible means. The greatest gratitude certainly belongs to my wife – you always stand by my side especially when things are not easy. Together with you, there seem no unreachable challenges. Te quiero mi media naranja!

Florian Geiger

Table of Contents

FOREWORD V
PREFACE VII
LIST OF TABLES XI
LIST OF FIGURES XII
LIST OF ABBREVIATIONS XIII
LIST OF SYMBOLS XIV
1 INTRODUCTION 1
2 THE INFLUENCE OF INDUSTRY CONCENTRATION ON MERGER MOTIVES 9
2.1 Introduction 9
2.2 Literature review and hypothesis development 13
2.2.1 Literature review on merger motives 13
2.2.2 Literature review on the influence of industry concentration 17
2.2.3 Hypothesis development 18
2.3 Data and methodology 21
2.3.1 Sample composition 21
2.3.2 Calculation of announcement period abnormal returns 24
2.3.3 Explanation of cross-sectional influence factors 25
2.4 Empirical results 30
2.4.1 Univariate analysis 30
2.4.2 Cross-sectional regression analysis 37
2.5 Summary and conclusion 43
3 CORPORATE RELATEDNESS AND WEALTH CREATION IN MACHINERY MERGERS 45
3.1 Introduction 45
3.2 Literature review, market characteristics, and hypothesis development 48
3.2.1 Literature review on relatedness 48
3.2.2 Market characteristics of the machinery industry 50
3.2.3 Hypothesis development 52
3.3 Data and methodology 54
3.3.1 Sample composition 54
3.3.2 Calculation of announcement period abnormal returns 55
3.3.3 Classification of relatedness 57

3.3.4 Explanation of cross-sectional influence factors ... 63
3.4 Empirical results ... 67
3.4.1 Univariate analysis ... 67
3.4.2 Cross-sectional regression analysis ... 72
3.5 Summary and conclusion ... 79
4 HORIZONTAL ACQUISITIONS, MERGER RENTS, AND NON-PRICE COMPETITION – A CASE STUDY FROM THE MACHINERY INDUSTRY ... 81
4.1 Introduction ... 81
4.2 Literature review and market characteristics ... 84
4.2.1 Literature review ... 84
4.2.2 Market characteristics of the metal forming industry ... 86
4.3 Case study background ... 89
4.3.1 Characterization of transaction partners ... 89
4.3.2 Discussion of merger motives and transaction synergies ... 91
4.3.3 Description of the acquisition event ... 94
4.3.4 Specification of the integration process ... 95
4.4 Acquisition performance ... 98
4.4.1 The capital market perspective ... 98
4.4.2 The operational performance analysis ... 104
4.4.2.1 Analysis of order income ... 104
4.4.2.2 Financial statement analysis ... 105
4.5 Summary and conclusion ... 109
5 CONCLUDING REMARKS ... 112
REFERENCES ... 115

List of Tables

Table 2.1 Summary of forecasted CAR reactions to different merger theories........16
Table 2.2 Sample selection and screening procedure...22
Table 2.3 Distribution of annual transactions and transaction volumes 23
Table 2.4 Variable definition and source description...28
Table 2.5 Descriptive statistics on continuous and binary variables.........................29
Table 2.6 Excess stock returns to machinery manufacturers...................................30
Table 2.7 Subsample analysis for concentrated/fragmented industries 33
Table 2.8 Subsample analysis for fragmented industries: high/low change HHI 35
Table 2.9 Multivariate analysis of acquirer abnormal returns 40
Table 2.10 Multivariate analysis of rival abnormal returns 42
Table 3.1 Descriptive statistics on continuous and binary variables.........................61
Table 3.2 Distribution of transactions by industry and transaction type...................62
Table 3.3 Variable definition and source description...65
Table 3.4 Excess stock returns to machinery manufacturers...................................67
Table 3.5 Subsample analysis relatedness – primary segments...............................68
Table 3.6 Subsample analysis relatedness – primary/secondary segments...............69
Table 3.7 Subsample analysis on forward and backward integration.......................71
Table 3.8 Multivariate analysis of acquirer CAR – primary segments.....................75
Table 3.9 Multivariate analysis of acquirer CAR – primary/secondary segments....77
Table 4.1 Short-term abnormal returns of MW, Schuler, and rival companies 101
Table 4.2 Long-term abnormal returns to Schuler – different approaches 103
Table 4.3 Overview absolute and relative quarterly order income Schuler............105
Table 4.4 Key profit & loss and balance sheet data of Schuler 106
Table 4.5 Selected performance indicators of Schuler...108

List of Figures

Figure 2.1 Short-term cumulative average abnormal returns....................................30
Figure 4.1 New organizational structure Schuler..96
Figure 4.2 Share price development Schuler and MW 2007.......................................99
Figure 4.3 Long-term share price development Schuler and indices 102

List of Abbreviations

AG	Aktiengesellschaft (listed company)
BH(A)R	Buy and hold (abnormal) return
bn	Billion
C(A)AR	Cumulative (average) abnormal return
CAGR	Cumulative average growth rate
CAPEX	Capital expenditure
CEO	Chief executive officer
CF	Cash-flow
CWE	Combined wealth effects
EBIT	Earnings before interest and taxes
EBITDA	Earnings before interest, taxes, depreciation, and
EBT	Earnings before taxes
GmbH	Gesellschaft mit beschränkter Haftung (limited company)
HHI	Herfindahl-Hirschman index
IO-table	Input-output table
kN	Kilo newton
Ltd.	Limited (limited company)
Log.	Logarithm
MW	Mueller Weingarten
m	Million
MtBV	Market to book value
M&A	Mergers and acquisitions
OLS	Ordinary least square
PoC	Percentage of completion
SCP	Structure-conduct-performance
Stdev.	Standard deviation
SIC	Standard industrial classification
OEM	Original equipment manufacturer
TEUR	Thousand Euros
US	United States

List of Symbols

$AR_{i,t}$	Abnormal return of share i at time t
a_{ij}	US-Dollar value of industry i's output required to produce industry j's total output
b_{ik}	Percentage of industry i's output supplied to intermediate industry k
$corr(b_{ik}, b_{jk})$	Correlation coefficient between of input/output between a pair of industries i and j
N	Number of observations
R^2	Coefficient of determination
$R_{m,t}$	Return on market index in time t (event period)
R_{it}	Return of share i at time t (event period)
$\bar{R}_m$	Average market return during estimation period
s_i	Variance of the residuals during estimation period
T_0	Event date
T_i	Number of days of security i in estimation period
v_{ij}	US-dollar value of industry i's output necessary to produce one US-dollar's worth of industry j's output

1 Introduction

During the last decade, the machinery industry has experienced major dynamics and changes of its market environment. Advancing innovation, changing client demands, shifting sales markets, increasing factor costs, and stronger price competition are just few trends that put increasing challenges on machinery manufacturers and that emphasize the need for technological, operational, and strategic realignment. In this context, machinery manufacturers have identified mergers and acquisitions (M&A) as an adequate strategy to adapt to the changing market requirements and demands (RBSC 2008). This is reflected in increasing M&A volumes in the machinery industry. In 2007, the global transaction volume was estimated at USD 65bn, a sixteen-fold increase compared to the year 1990. During the same period, the number of transactions increased only by factor 2.5 reflecting a growing average deal size of transactions. The growing importance of M&A transactions also continued in recent years with a volume increase of 36 percent from 2006 to 2007.

The theoretical foundation for firms to engage in mergers has long been entrenched by financial and strategic literature and includes both, theories on merger motivation as well as on merger consequences. Those theories range from efficiency considerations (Rumelt 1974; Walker 2000), market power views (Stigler 1964; Sharur 2005), transaction cost arguments (Coase 1937; Williamson 1979; Crocker 1983), property rights (Grossman and Hart 1986; Hart and Moore 1990; Ordover, Saloner, and Salop 1990), and risk based explanations (Amihud and Lev 1981; Seth 1990) to agency and hubris theories (Montgomery 1994). However, final answers whether mergers, from an empirical and economic perspective, have to be evaluated positively cannot be given definitely. In fact, the suggested theoretical benefits are often not reflected in a large body of empirical research which states instead that mergers often fail to generate value for shareholders and/or fail to realize the expected synergies (Pautler 2003; Ficery, Herd, and Pursche 2007). For practitioners and academic researchers it is therefore sometimes difficult to draw the right conclusions (Brunner 2002).

One reason for ambiguous results is probably that study designs often do not adequately consider industry-specific trends and market developments that may severely influence M&A transactions (Fowler and Schmidt 1988; Mitchell and Mulherin 1996).[1] By concentrating on the machinery industry, we overcome the methodological shortcomings of broader empirical studies allowing to account for industry-specific logics, trends, and conditions. Furthermore, the machinery industry, compared to other industries, offers unique characteristics that demand for a thorough analysis and understanding of M&A motives and consequences:

(1) The machinery industry is a heterogeneous compound of various sub-industries. This fragmentation results in different market structures, economic dependencies, and influence factors within an sufficiently homogenous industry environment.

(2) Discussions on the appropriate corporate focus and diversification strategy are especially strong in the machinery industry because of heterogeneous business strategies of market participants (from large, integrated conglomerates to specialized, single-business firms).

(3) With an estimated worldwide market volume of approximately USD 1,850bn in 2007, the importance of the machinery industry in global economies is significant. It accounts for a high proportion of economic outputs and plays an important role as driver of global development through innovations and technological advancements (Bureau of Economic Analysis 2008; VDMA 2008).

These considerations on industry-specific characteristics and economic relevance of machinery mergers are the starting point for my doctoral thesis which consists of three papers. To gain insights into the nature and impact of M&A transactions in the

[1] Although the analysis of the impact of merger activity on shareholder value has generated a vast amount of academic research, results are to some extent contradictory as industrial dynamics and trends are difficult to compare across industries. This finding seems to be considered in a growing amount of industry-specific econometric analyses.

machinery industry, I choose a top-down approach evaluating first motives and benefits of machinery mergers (section 2), before examining imminent wealth mechanics and value drivers (section 3). Then, I provide additional insights into merger rent generation on a case study basis (section 4). In the following, I briefly discuss the key research questions that are examined in this thesis.

First research question:[2]

The relationship between market structure and firm performance has been well examined in industrial organization research. Based on traditional views of Schumpeter (1912) and Bain (1954), industry concentration is acknowledged to influence profits, innovation dynamics, risk behavior, and asset pricing of firms (Almazan and Molina 2002; Knott and Hart 2003; Slade 2004; MacKay and Phillips 2005; Hou and Robinson 2006). By linking to industrial organization theory, we argue that motives of firms to engage in mergers should be influenced by their prevailing industry environment. Merger decisions arise from an equilibrium in product markets that potentially reflect strategic interactions among market participants. As the structure of product markets may affect, for example, the risk of firms' cash flows and investment decisions (Hou and Robinson 2006), firms' underlying rationale to engage in mergers should be influenced correspondingly. While the impact of market structures on corporate performance has been well entrenched in previous research, there is little evidence to enlighten the implications of industry structures on merger motives. We want to close this research gap by empirically analyzing implications of industry concentration on implicitly expressed merger motives of firms. Concentrating on the machinery industry, we overcome methodological shortcomings of cross-industry empirical studies (Fowler and Schmidt 1988; Mitchell and Mulherin 1996) allowing to assume a basic homogeneity of prevailing market trends and developments. In contrast to other industries, the machinery industry is highly

---

[2] A modified version of this paper will be published by Geiger and Schiereck (2008) in an international business journal.

fragmented providing sufficient heterogeneous market structures in its sub-segments allowing for a thorough examination of the influence of industry concentration on merger motives.

We indirectly test underlying merger motives under different conditions of industry concentration examining wealth effects of target, acquirer, combined entity, and rivals (Eckbo 1983; Stillmann 1983; Trautwein 1990; Fee and Thomas 2004; Sharur 2005) as well as by comparing correlations between acquirer excess returns and change of industry concentration (Ghosh 2004). Depending on the underlying industry concentration, we observe significant different capital market reactions among merger announcements suggesting that different takeover motives prevail in fragmented and concentrated industries. In contrast to previous studies, we find in fragmented industries, in addition to efficiency motives, evidence for monopolistic collusion. While mergers in concentrated industries seem primarily motivated to achieve efficiency and synergy gains, the absence of collusion motives may be an indication for a successful enforcement of antitrust legislation. Our results suggest that the impact of industry concentration may have been under-estimated in previous empirical research on merger motives which may have led to a potential distortion of results.

Second research question:[3]

Corporate vertical integration and diversification strategies are fundamental topics in strategic management research. Empirical research agrees that the right corporate focus contributes to wealth generation in mergers and that diversified companies trade at a discount (Lang and Stulz 1994; Servaes 1996; Denis, Denis, and Yost 2002). Brunner (2002) states in his literature review on profitability implications of mergers:

---

[3] A modified version of this paper will be published by Geiger, Schiereck, Wald (2009) in an international business journal.

"Value is created by focus, relatedness, and adherence to strategy [...]. Diversification destroys value [...] The key implication of these insights is that managers can make choices that materially influence the profitability of M&A."

However, recent critics highlight the influence of sample selection effects (Campa and Kedia 2002; Gomes and Livdan 2004), the disregard of different industry logics (Fowler and Schmidt 1988; Mitchell and Mulherin 1996), and methodological shortcoming of relatedness classification (Fan and Goyal 2006). We shed additional light on this discussion providing a detailed industry-specific perspective examining merger decisions of machinery firms for various degrees of relatedness. Reviewing dominating industry trends, we show that discussion on corporate focus and diversification seems especially important for machinery manufacturers. This is reflected in the heterogeneous business strategies of market participants (from large, integrated conglomerates to specialized, single-business firms) making the machinery industry particularly suitable to scrutinize different merger decisions. To account for the complexity of relatedness classification in empirical studies, we use commodity flow data (input-output data) to construct quantitative measures of relatedness (Fan and Lang 2000; Fan and Goyal 2006). Applying this approach, we capture the relation between a pair of merging firms from the dollar amount of input transfer between the industries in which the merging firms operate.

The results of our study highlight the benefits of corporate focus in merger situations confirming a generally positive relationship between corporate relatedness and excess returns. However, findings also suggest that the discussion on corporate focus should account for vertical value chain implications. We find that vertical upstream mergers show similar positive returns as horizontal transactions supporting benefits such as control over subsequent stages of production, influence on demand, improvements of product offerings, as well as an increase in flexibility. In most empirical research on corporate focus this strongly value contributing aspect seems not sufficiently considered. Our results also show positive abnormal return implications for acquirer shareholders in lateral transactions rejecting the proposition that diversification destroys value. Moreover, our findings underline the importance of individual target and acquirer characteristics as wealth determinants in merger transactions emphasizing the firm's abilities and experiences of target selection and target integration.

Third research question:[4]

Direct claims that a merger is made to achieve market power are rare, as collusive synergies are often seen as attempts of merging firms to expropriate wealth from customers by limiting output, raising product prices and/or lowering factor prices (Stigler 1964; Chatterjee 1986; Trautwein 1990; Sharur 2005). This makes it difficult for economic researchers with their coarse information set to really understand the implicit nature of market power synergies (Andrade, Mitchell, and Stafford 2001; Pautler 2001). We circumvent the methodological shortcomings of larger empirical studies and examine the sources and mechanics of market power effects by focusing on the merger of Schuler and Mueller Weingarten, two leading players in the metal forming industry.

This case study illustrates the role of non-price variables in competition and transaction synergies. The acquisition of Mueller Weingarten by Schuler in March 2007 created a new global leader in the metal forming industry with clear competitive advantage in technological know-how and innovation. With this transaction, Schuler was able to reduce existing strong price competition in the market and turn competition parameters towards non-price variables. This resulted in significant market power gains and merger rents through pricing effects in the market. Highlighting a large overall impact of transaction synergies, the merger showed strongly positive capital market evaluation and development of key accounting figures for Schuler. In contrast, rival companies experienced negative returns and decreasing relative accounting

[4] A modified version of this paper will be published by Geiger and Schiereck (2009) in an international business journal.

performance. This observation contradicts existing research that interprets collusive mergers as being related to positive competitor developments, as rival firms should profit from limited outputs and increased product prices (Eckbo 1983; Chatterjee 1986; Fee and Thomas 2004; Sharur 2005). We interpret the results in two ways. First, mergers that allow for gaining significant competitive advantages in non-price variables are highly efficient in realizing shareholder wealth gains through increased market power. Second, contrary to theoretical evidence, we show that market power rents in form of pricing advantages are not necessarily available to industry rivals when markets compete in non-price variables. We believe that this is especially true in know-how and service intense industries.

This doctoral thesis contributes to financial research, industrial organization theory and strategic management research. On the one hand, each paper adds additional perspectives on the growing body of industry-related merger research and corporate decision making. The first paper closes a substantial research gap by providing evidence for the influence of industry concentration on merger motives and by highlighting the interdependence of industrial organization theory and financial research. The results provided in the second paper add to the ongoing discussion about the adequate strategy of firms with regard to the right business model. I suggest that the discussion on the appropriate corporate focus needs to include decisions on value chain integration strategies of firms. Finally, the third paper, based on a case study analysis, allows a more thorough understanding of market power rents, wealth mechanics, and post-merger integration success. On the other hand, next to addressing substantial theoretical and empirical research gaps, my work may prove to be relevant for practitioners and investment professionals, as motivations, drivers, wealth determinants, and benefits of machinery mergers are discussed. In a top-down approach, I evaluate merger motives and associated benefits in the machinery industry, explain underlying wealth mechanics and business model implications, and discuss specific wealth determinants and merger rents. Both, my theoretical and the related empirical evidence provided on transaction evaluations, may serve as a starting point and guideline for future merger decisions in the machinery industry.

2 The Influence of Industry Concentration on Merger Motives

2.1 Introduction

Although the influence of market structure on corporate performance and merger success has long been outlined by the industrial organization theory, only little is known about its specific impact on merger motives. Following recommendations of merger motive research, we examine stock price reactions of merging firms and rival companies to transaction announcements to generate an understanding of how industry concentration influences merger decisions and merger motives of firms.

Firms' motives to engage in mergers should be influenced by their prevailing market environment. Merger decisions arise from an equilibrium in product markets that potentially reflect strategic interactions among market participants. As the structure of product markets may affect, for example, the risk of a firm's cash flows and consequently firm's investment decisions, its underlying rationale to engage in mergers should be influenced correspondingly. We argue similar as Hou and Robinson (2006), who assume that industry concentration influences the risk behavior of firms, an development of traditional views of Schumpeter (1912) and Bain (1954). In their line of argument, industry concentration influences innovation dynamics, firm's distress risk, and directly impacts the process of creative destruction. Linking to industrial organization theory that highlights the determination of endogenous market conduct by exogenous market factors, we argue that this influence should also be reflected in strategic merger motives of firms. For example, as innovation dynamics and efficiency pressure increase in competitive industries (Knott and Hart 2003), mergers in this industry environment should primarily be motivated by efficiency gains in form of operational, managerial, or financial synergies. In contrast, mergers in concentrated industries should be primarily driven by monopolistic collusion motives, as tendencies to limit output, raise product prices, and/or lower factor prices appear more promising (Chatterjee 1986). Capital markets should recognize this impact of industry concentration by evaluating those transactions differently.

We test for three lines of reasoning that explain merger motives: First, the efficiency theory which suggests mergers are motivated by synergies and that wealth creation depends on the operational and strategic fit of both companies. Second, the monopolistic collusion theory which argues that mergers are executed to improve market positioning and to achieve market power. Third, the agency and hubris theories that assume either agency problems in the form of wealth transfers between acquiring and target shareholders or hubris of management through overestimation of potential synergies and overpayment of the target. We indirectly test for efficiency, collusion, and hubris hypotheses under different conditions of market structure (concentrated and fragmented markets) examining wealth effects of target, acquirer, combined entity, and rival firms (Eckbo 1983; Stillmann 1983; Trautwein 1990; Fee and Thomas 2004; Sharur 2005) as well as by comparing correlations between acquirer excess returns and change of industry concentration (Ghosh 2004). Following this method, we are able to examine how specific industry characteristics influence merger motives of management.

Based on 330 M&A transactions between 1997 to 2007, our analysis focuses specifically on the machinery industry for three reasons. First, reviewing the amount of empirical research, it seems that a cross-industry analysis may fall too short to consider specific industry-related market developments and trends. In fact, general market trends across industries (e.g. banking, telecommunications or pharmaceuticals) are difficult to compare.[5] Concentrating on one industry, we overcome the methodological short-comings of broader empirical studies and we can assume a basic homogeneity of prevailing market trends and developments. Second, in contrast to other industries, the machinery industry is highly fragmented providing sufficient heterogeneous market

---

[5] Although the analysis of the impact of merger activity on shareholder value has generated a vast amount of academic research, results are to some extent contradictory as industrial dynamics and trends are hard to compare across industries. This finding seems to be considered in a growing amount of industry-specific econometric analyses.

structures allowing a thorough examination of the influence of industry concentration on merger motives. Following the Standard Industrial Classification (SIC) system, the heterogeneity of the market is reflected in 37 different sub-industries where nine industries are classified as concentrated industries (Herfindahl-Hirschman index > 0.18).[6] Similarly, the US Census Bureau (2002) confirms the market fragmentation stating that the largest 20 machinery manufacturers in US equal an aggregate of 27.8 percent market share compared to 56.3 percent in commercial banking or 78.8 percent in telecommunications. Third, the machinery industry, often cited as driver of the economy, is one of the most important sectors worldwide with a global production output of more than USD 1,850bn in 2007 (Bureau of Economic Analysis 2008; VDMA 2008). The importance of this industry alone should have put machinery in the spotlight of academic research, however, until now there is only limited knowledge in this area. These three arguments make the machinery industry particularly suitable for the examination of our research question.

Using univariate and cross-sectional analysis, we find support for our hypothesis that industry concentration influences merger motives of firms. Interpreting capital market reactions to transaction announcements, we observe significantly different abnormal return reactions for rival firms in fragmented and concentrated industries. Complementing abnormal return analysis with the correlation approach developed by Ghosh (2004), we reject monopolistic collusion motives for concentrated industries, as the observed negative rival reaction can only be explained by competitive disadvantages resulting from productive efficiency gains of the merging firms. In fragmented industries, we detect evidence for both, productive efficiency motives and monopolistic collusions motives. There are no indications for agency and hubris motives, as acquirer returns are positive and no wealth transfers between shareholders are observed. Results from cross-sectional analyses confirm the direct influence of the contingency variable industry concentration. Furthermore, findings indicate that wealth

---

6 For example, the market for manufacturing printing machines (SIC 3555) is dominated by a limited number of rivals, each with high market shares. On the other hand, markets such as machine tools manufacturing (SIC 3541) are highly fragmented and characterized by low market concentration.

creation mechanics of acquirer, target, and rivals differ for transactions in concentrated and fragmented industries. Considering value maximizing behavior of management, those differences should consequently lead to different merger motives and merger strategies of firms.

The remainder of the paper is structured as follows. In section 2.2, we first provide an overview of the current strand of merger motive research, before we illuminate current notions of the industrial organization theory. Summarizing those findings, we derive our research hypotheses. In section 2.3, we provide descriptive statistics on our sample, identify factors that can explain observed wealth effects of the transactions, and discuss our econometric model. In section 2.4, we conduct both univariate and multivariate analyses to identify determinants of wealth effects and their impact on merger motives. More specifically, we examine whether excess returns of transactions in fragmented or concentrated industries have different cross-sectional determinants of merger success. We conclude with a discussion of our findings in section 2.5.

2.2 Literature review and hypothesis development

2.2.1 Literature review on merger motives

Although the decision to merge is often driven by a complex pattern of motives that cannot be put into one single approach, research has developed some general theories to explain driving forces and assumptions behind mergers. However, a final answer has not been found, as it is difficult for economic researchers to identify the sources of gains with their coarse information set (Andrade, Mitchell, and Stafford 2001). This paper tries to shed additional light on the topic by suggesting that the influence of industry concentration should be considered in the research of merger motives. In the following, we briefly introduce three major merger theories and explain how these motives can be identified by observing capital market reactions of stakeholder firms.

The first theory is the efficiency theory (also called synergy theory). It stipulates that mergers are executed to achieve synergies in form of financial synergies (lower cost of capital), operational synergies (combination of operations and knowledge transfer), and/or managerial synergies (when the acquirer possesses superior management skills and abilities). In fact, synergies are often cited as a key argument to improve productive efficiency and to justify management actions (Porter 1987; Ficery, Herd, and Pursche 2007; Phillips 2008). Capron (1999) argues that cost synergies are often driven by asset divestitures (physical assets and cutback of personnel) while revenue-enhancing synergies emphasize the redeployment of resources to improve the company's ability to generate earnings. Empirical research shows that a relationship between the net present value of synergies and announcement day return exists, although revenue-enhancing synergies are not valued as highly as cost reduction synergies (Comment and Jarrell 1995; Walker 2000; Houston, James, and Ryngaert 2001). In an analysis of horizontal mergers, Fee and Thomas (2004) find evidence consistent with improved productive efficiency and buying power as sources of gains to acquirer firms. Similarly, Andrade and Stafford (2004) observe that mergers are effective means for industries with excess capacity to rationalize (cost synergies) and induce exit (divestitures).

To identify efficiency motives in mergers, empirical research suggests to examine capital market reactions (Eckbo 1983; Fee and Thomas 2004; Sharur 2005; Chatterjee 2007). According to literature the positive impact of synergies and efficiency gains is reflected in positive capital market evaluations for target and acquiring companies following the merger announcement. In contrast, share price reactions of rival companies are not clearly determinable as both, positive and negative excess returns, are allegeable. For example, if the merging parties achieve a more efficient production or market positioning, rival companies should experience negative stock returns as they perceive competitive disadvantages (Schumann 1993). The opposite effect occurs if the merger induces a positive signal to the market indicating that rival firms are able to copy the efficiency gain of the merging companies (e.g. better production routines) or that the probability increases that the rivals themselves will become targets (Akhigbe, Borde, and Whyte 2000; Song and Walkling 2000).

The second theory is the monopolistic collusion theory which argues that mergers (horizontal and conglomerate mergers) are executed to improve market positioning and to gain market power. Trautwein (1990) summarizes that the monopoly theory's evidence appears to be weak, as most studies show that the primary reason for mergers is not to achieve monopoly power. This is confirmed by recent evidence. For example, Fee and Thomas (2004) find in their investigation of upstream and downstream product-market effects only little indication for monopolistic collusion. Also Shahrur (2005) rejects collusion motives examining a sample of horizontal takeovers. Nonetheless, we test for evidence on monopoly consequences of mergers by observing target, acquirer, and rival capital market reactions around the merger announcement date.

As an improved market power may be achieved through collusive mergers, there should be a positive wealth gain observable for target and acquirer shareholders. Rival firms should also benefit (positive abnormal return reaction) since the positioning of all companies in the industry is improved through a tendency to limit output, raise product prices and/or lower factor prices (Chatterjee 1986). However, a positive rival reaction itself cannot entirely prove monopolistic collusion motives (Stillmann 1983; Eckbo and Wier 1985). Consequently, we apply an additional approach to strengthen the interpretation of results and to distinguish between underlying efficiency and competitive collusion motives. Following an approach by Ghosh (2004), a positive correlation between shareholder wealth gains and changes in industry concentration is a suitable indicator for the market power theory. Hence, a positive correlation in combination with abnormal return analysis of deal participants should allow a reliable evaluation and interpretation of merger motives.

The third line of reasoning focuses on analyzing why mergers sometimes destroy wealth of acquirer shareholders. It includes the agency theory (managers who maximize their own utility) and hubris theory (overestimation of management's abilities). Empirical studies show that at least part of the often significant share price increase of target firms is attributed to a general wealth transfer from acquirer to target. For example, Walking and Long (1984) find that the existence or absence of managerial resistance to a takeover bid is directly related to the target management's personal wealth change induced by takeovers. Also Roll (1986) explains managers' behavior to not abandon unfavorable takeover offers with hubris, even since reflection would suggest that such bids are likely to represent positive errors in valuation. Seyhun (1990) reports value destruction for acquiring firms in mergers and concludes that takeovers are motivated by agency problems or hubris. Malmendier and Tate (2002) measure hubris by the options a manager has left unexercised and find evidence that overconfident managers make more acquisitions while abnormal returns are generally lower. We test for the hubris or agency motive by assessing whether negative acquirer returns are observed and/or a wealth transfer between target and acquirer shareholder exists.

Although in literature there are other theories such as the process theory (limited information, organizational routines, and political power) or the disturbance theory (merger waves are caused by economic disturbances), we focus on the initially introduced lines of argument (efficiency/synergy, monopolistic collusion, and agency/hubris motives) following preceding research examples (Eckbo 1983; Berkovitch and Narayanan 1993; Sharur 2005).[7] Table 2.1 summarizes expected capital market reactions to cumulative abnormal returns of target, bidder, combined entity, and rivals according to the different introduced merger theories.

Table 2.1 Summary of forecasted CAR reactions to different merger theories

This table summarizes the implications of several merger theories on the cumulative abnormal returns of target, acquirer, combined entity, and rival shareholders in line with Shahrur (2005). It allows to interpret results from the event study analysis of machinery manufacturers with regard to underlying merger motives.

Merger theory	Forecasted influence on CARs			
	Target	Acquirer	Combined Entity	Rivals
Efficiency/synergy theory (maximization of target and acquirer gains)	Positive (bargaining power)	Positive (synergies and lower costs)	Positive (synergies and lower costs)	Unclear[1)] (positive signal versus compet. advantage)
Monopoly theory (improved market positioning and market power)	Positive (bargaining power)	Positive (monopoly rent)	Positive (monopoly rent)	Positive[1)] (market structure)
Agency theory (maximization of own utility)	Positive (bargaining power)	Negative (misbehavior of management)	Zero to negative	Zero to positive (no competitive advantage)
Hubris theory (overvaluation of target potentials)	Positive (bargaining power)	Negative (overvaluation of synergies)	Slightly positive	Zero to positive (no competitive advantage)

1) As positive rival reactions are not sufficient to separate efficiency motives from monopoly motives, we test also for correlation of acquirer CARs and change in industry concentration (Ghosh 2004).

7 For more information, refer to the summary on merger motives by Trautwein (1990).

2.2.2 *Literature review on the influence of industry concentration*

This paper is part of a larger literature linking industrial organization theory to financial research. While most research links the influence of industrial organization to company performance, to the best of our knowledge, this is the first work to specifically analyze the impact on corporate decision making in merger situations.

One of the key questions industrial organization theory tries to answer is how market structures influence performance and profitability of firms. Empirical research confirms a relationship between market structure and firm profitability, although results are often weak (Weiss 1974). One model for explaining firm performance is the structure-conduct-performance (SCP) paradigm (Slade 2004). The SCP holds that exogenous market structure (in our case industry concentration) determines endogenous market conduct (the way in which the firms interact in that industry) which in turn determines firm performance (profitability). Although this model has been criticized including arguments that cause and effect are backwards (Demsetz 1973) and that cross-industry differences in profits are sometimes not positively related to market structure (Hirschey 1985; Rumelt 1991), recent research has resumed the discussion about the influence of industry characteristics on firm performance. For example, in his empirical analysis of 14 nonferrous-metal mining and refining markets, Slade (2004) finds strong support for the SCP model. Firms profits are positively and significantly related to the structure of their markets and this relationship holds true for all specifications that are estimated. Similar evidence is also provided by Azzam (1997) in an analysis of the US beef packing industry. He empirically confirms the trade-off between market power and cost efficiency from increased concentration. Morrison Paul (2003) provides evidence of substantive cost economies implying economic motivations for industry concentration, consolidation, and diversification.

There is increasing research examining the impact of industry components on risk behavior, capital structure, and asset pricing. In a first work to explore the link between the influence of industry concentration on average stock returns, Hou and Robinson

(2006) offer empirical evidence of asset pricing implications. Their analysis proves that firms in more concentrated industries earn lower returns assuming that high industry concentration either insulates firms from undiversifiable distress risk through high barriers to entry or decreases their risk behavior because they engage in less innovation and thereby command lower expected returns. MacKay and Philipps (2005) find that financial structure, technology, and risk are jointly determined within industries. In competitive industries, financial leverage seems higher and less dispersed. Almazan and Molina (2002) confirm the impact of industry characteristics, observing that differences of firms' capital structures are greater in industries that are highly concentrated. In his examination of lead-lag effects,[8] Hou (2003) supports the idea that certain asset-pricing phenomena are attributable to industry effects.

In accordance with the SCP-model, we conclude that market structure (exogenous factor) appears to influence firm performance (endogenous factor). We indirectly transfer this relationship to merger situations of firms. By measuring wealth creation in mergers (performance) and the exogenous factor of industry concentration (structure), we examine how endogenous market conduct (in our case merger motives) is influenced. Similar to Hou and Robinson (2006) and Curry and George (1983), we focus on industry concentration as a key determinant of underlying market structures.

2.2.3 Hypothesis development

Assuming that certain merger motives or strategies are in different industry environments more value contributing than others, we presume that industry concentration should influence management's merger motives. As suggested by literature, we identify underlying merger motives by observing different capital market reactions of acquirer, target, and rival firms (compare table 2.1). As we do not expect hubris or agency motives being dominating in merger decisions, return developments

[8] The lead-lag effect describes the situation where one (leading) variable is correlated with the value of another (lagging) variable at later times.

should be positive for target and acquirer shareholders. However, we only make assumptions on the sources of gains, but not the magnitude of it. Consequently, our hypothesis does not suggest that, in dependence of underlying industry environments (concentrated and fragmented industries), there should be a substantial difference in the magnitude of acquirer and/or target abnormal returns.

Hypothesis I: In the absence of wealth transfers, target and acquirer wealth creation is positive. Furthermore, the magnitude of target and acquirer wealth creation is not substantially influenced by different levels of industry concentration.

For rival reactions we expect different reactions. According to the discussed merger theories above, the direction of rival excess returns depends on underlying merger motives of firms. Therefore, if we observe different capital market reactions for rival firms in dependence of industry concentration, we associate this signal with varying merger motives. In expectation of this industry influence, we hypothesize that rival reactions should react differently in concentrated and fragmented industries.

Hypothesis II: Capital market reactions of rival companies are substantially different for fragmented and concentrated industries.

A confirmation of these hypotheses allows a further examination of the logic and relationship of industry concentration on merger motives. As discussed, concentrated industries allow their market participants to benefit from dominant market positioning where firms can leverage scale advantages and are able to limit output, raise product prices and/or lower factor prices (Chatterjee 1986). The ability to realize collusive rents in concentrated industries seems therefore more promising. Additionally, existing research shows that market pressure and competition for innovation dynamics and efficiency leadership is lower in concentrated industries (Knott and Hart 2003). Consequently, we hypothesize that mergers in concentrated industries should primarily be motivated by monopolistic collusion.

Hypothesis III: In concentrated industries, monopolistic collusion motives dominate merger decisions. This is identified by positive abnormal returns of targets, acquirers, and rival firms as well as a positive correlation of acquirer abnormal returns and changes of industry concentration.

Following Porter (1985), a higher number of competitors results in higher diversity of strategies, capabilities, and market segmentation within an industry. Barney (1997) argues that increasing fragmentation results in increased strategic uncertainty, higher mortality rates, and efficiency pressures for firms. Knott and Hart (2003) conclude that competitive pressure is especially strong in fragmented industries, hence, synergies in form of financial, operational, or managerial improvements should be primary motives for merger transactions. In contrast to concentrated industries, it seems more difficult in fragmented industries to achieve potential gains from monopolistic collusion, as the overall transaction impact seems low. Our hypothesis is as follows.

Hypothesis IV: Fragmented industries strive primarily for efficiency improvements and synergy effects in merger situations. This is identified by positive target and acquirer gains, and a non-correlation of acquirer abnormal returns and changes of industry concentration.

Through univariate and cross-sectional analysis, we validate our hypotheses on the influence of industry concentration on management's merger motives.

2.3 Data and methodology

2.3.1 Sample composition

Our sample includes mergers and acquisitions from the Thomson One Banker deal database announced globally between January 1, 1997 and December 31, 2007 that fulfill the following requirements:

(1) The acquirer is a machinery manufacturer and has sufficient stock information available.
(2) The transaction is a majority investment (>50 percent share after deal completion).
(3) The deal value is at least USD 20 million.
(4) Transactions by one acquirer do not overlap within the estimation period of 250 days.
(5) The acquirer's primary SIC code is not part of computer equipment and office machines.
(6) Transaction details are confirmed by Factiva press research.

Between 1997 and 2007 more than 5.700 M&A transactions are reported for the machinery industry. For the purpose of this study, several selection criteria are applied to refine the sample. By applying criterion (1), we include only transactions where sufficient stock market data is available to estimate abnormal returns via the market model. Criterion (2) and (3) ensure that the impact of the transaction on both acquirer and target company is above a specified minimum threshold, in order to assure that merger motives are sufficiently reflected in deal participant's and rival's share price reactions. To maximize the reliability of our data sample, we exclude transactions with overlapping M&A transactions in the observation period (criterion 4). To focus on machinery manufacturers only, we exclude all companies under the SIC classification computer manufacturing (criterion 5).[9] We confirm each of the remaining transactions by screening news articles from the Factiva database for misspecification (criterion 6). Applying criteria (1) to (6) we yield a total sample of 330 transactions. Table 2.2 and 2.3 highlight in detail the screening process and provide information about the annual distribution of the transactions.

Table 2.2 Sample selection and screening procedure

This table shows the total number of completed M&A transactions with target or acquirer mid description machinery over the period from 1997-2007 initially obtained from the SDC/Thomson One Banker deal database and the final data set after application of the defined selection criteria (1)-(6). The selection criteria are: (1) acquirer mid description is machinery manufacturer and relevant Datastream codes are available for acquirers; (2) the transaction is a majority investment (> 50 percent share in the target company) while no majority stake was owned before; (3) the relevant deal value is at least USD 20m; (4) transactions within the same estimation period (250 days) of one acquirer are corrected; (5) The acquirer's primary SIC Code is within the two digit SIC Code 35, furthermore eliminating all transactions related to computer equipment and office machines (three-digit SIC-Code "357"); (6) transaction details are confirmed by Factiva research.

Screening criteria	Number of transactions	% of reported transactions
Total Machinery M&A transactions (1997-2007)	5,753	100.0%
Screened after criterion (1)	2,899	50.4%
Screened after criterion (2)	2,291	39.8%
Screened after criterion (3)	485	8.4%
Screened after criterion (4)	395	6.9%
Screened after criterion (5)	348	6.0%
Screened after criterion (6)	330	5.7%

9 We excluded 3570 computer & office equipment, 3571 electronic computers, 3572 computer storage devices, 3575 computer terminals, 3576 computer communication equipment, 3577 computer peripheral equipment.

Table 2.3 Distribution of annual transactions and transaction volumes

This table shows the annual distribution of the analyzed transactions and transaction volumes between 1997 and 2007.

Year	Number of transactions	Percentage	Transaction Volume	Percentage
1997	42	12.7%	8,126	10.2%
1998	36	10.9%	3,541	4.4%
1999	38	11.5%	13,696	17.2%
2000	30	9.1%	3,504	4.4%
2001	16	4.8%	1,630	2.0%
2002	18	5.5%	2,763	3.5%
2003	25	7.6%	4,603	5.8%
2004	23	7.0%	5,017	6.3%
2005	30	9.1%	6,604	8.3%
2006	30	9.1%	19,550	24.5%
2007	42	12.7%	10,634	13.3%
Total	**330**	**100.0%**	**79,668**	**100.0%**

To examine rival reactions to merger announcements, we identify relevant rival firms from the Thomson One Banker Peer Analysis database. We consider any company as a rival company (besides the bidder and target) that reports its primary four-digit SIC code in the industry where acquirer and target company overlap. If there is no overlap, we use the primary SIC code segment of the acquirer to test for rival reactions. For the rival portfolio, we include all companies with revenues greater than USD 1 million where sufficient share data is available from Datastream. We observe reactions of 880 rival firms in our sample. For the average deal, we identify 23 rival firms to calculate announcement period abnormal returns in a value weighted portfolio.

To measure industry concentration, we compute a sales-based Herfindahl-Hirschman index (HHI) in the industry where acquirer's and target's four-digit SIC-codes overlap (Hou and Robinson 2006). Calculating industry concentration measures requires detailed information regarding market share of firms in each sub-industry. We obtain the data using the Thomson One Banker database which also includes information on privately held companies.[10] Following the guidelines of the US Antitrust Division of the Department of Justice, we consider all industries with an HHI greater than 0.18 as highly concentrated.

2.3.2 *Calculation of announcement period abnormal returns*

We use standard event study methodology to calculate abnormal returns for target, bidder, combined entity, as well as rival companies applying the standard market model as derived by Brown and Warner (1985). We estimate abnormal returns to firm i at date t (AR_{it}) as $AR_{it} = R_{it} - \alpha_i - \beta_i R_{mt}$, where R_{mt} is the return of the relevant country-specific Datastream machinery index.[11] Our market model parameters are estimated over an observation period of 250 trading days starting at day T_{-300} to T_{-50} relative to the announcement date T_0. We exclude all companies with less trading days from our sample. We use the announcement date as reported by Thomson One Banker and cross-check the data using press research from Factiva. To obtain the cumulative abnormal return (CAR) of a transaction, we perform an ordinary leased squared (OLS) regression over six different event windows ranging between two days [-1;+1] and 20 days [-10;+10] around the announcement date. We estimate combined wealth effects (CWE) of merging companies as the cumulative abnormal return (CAR) to a value weighted portfolio of acquirer and target (Bradley, Desai, and Kim 1988). We weight the merging firms with their respective market values of equity for day T_{-21} relative to the announcement date. To estimate CARs for rival companies, we create value weighted rival portfolios (excluding acquirer and target) for the relevant four-digit SIC code where bidder and target overlap.

---

[10] The exclusion of private company information yields similar results.

[11] Abnormal returns are the difference between the expected return and the actual return observed in the market.

To test for statistical significance of the cumulated abnormal returns, we follow the recommendation of Harrington and Shrider (2007) and apply the test statistics of Boehmer, Musumeci, and Poulsen (1991), an enhancement of the approach developed by Patell (1976). The test considers the likely difference in cross-sectional return variance between the estimation period from T_{-300} to T_{-50} and the event window. The test statistic follows a student t-distribution with T-2 degrees of freedom. The test results appear to be robust in the absence of event-induced variance increases (Serra 2004).

2.3.3 Explanation of cross-sectional influence factors

We analyze the influence of industry concentration on merger motives by measuring determinants of wealth creation through several cross-sectional factors that are closely related to industry characteristics. We furthermore include some standard control variables to examine whether capital market reactions are related to generally applied determinants of merger success and to test whether value generation mechanics are different in fragmented and concentrated industries. We include three different sets of characteristics: industry, deal, and acquirer characteristics.

We hypothesize that industry characteristics determine merger motives and capital market reactions of mergers. Research has shown that industry concentration plays an important part in determining market power, business behavior, and company performance (Curry and George 1983) and that it is a suitable measure of barriers to entry (Hou and Robinson 2006). For our analysis, we measure market concentration as a sales-based Herfindahl-Hirschman index and use it as indicator for classifying sub-industries. We include a dummy variable (1 = concentrated, if HHI > 0.18) to test for the effects of market concentration and to perform univariate subsample analysis. For cross-sectional regression, we use metric measures of industry concentration. Second, we include industry growth as a variable in our analysis. By analyzing industry growth rates, we control for underlying industry dynamics. According to Clelland, Douglas, and Henderson (2006), there will be a higher level of competition in an industry with a lower growth rate reflecting an increasingly zero-sum game of mutual dependence. The lower the growth rate, the greater the intensity of competition between firms and the greater the influence on the relationship between value creation and its efficacy in producing a competitive advantage. We calculate growth rates based on data we obtain through the Thomson One Banker database measuring industry growth as average growth over three years before the merger announcement (CAGR). As third industry variable, we include the CAR of the rival/acquirer firm in order to measure the merger impact on the industry. We believe that there exists mutual dependence of acquirer abnormal returns and wealth impact on rival firms, as higher positive or negative rival reactions should influence acquirer returns and vice versa. We include abnormal acquirer/rival returns in corresponding event windows.

As deal variables we include standard control variables to test whether determinants of wealth creation are similar in fragmented and concentrated industries. First, the deal size of the transaction seems to influence potential merger implications for acquirer and target firms, as a higher transaction size may result in e.g. higher synergies and/or may facilitate monopolistic collusion. For example, Cornett, McNutt, and Tehranian (2006) find in an analysis of the banking industry that large bank mergers are associated with greater performance than small bank mergers. Wilcox, Chang, and Grover (2001) report the same for an analysis in the telecommunications industry. Helwege, Pirinsky, and Stulz (2007) explain this with the level of information asymmetries that decrease with firm size, as larger firms are more frequently monitored by analysts, institutional investors, and regulators. In contrast, Moeller, Schlingemann, and Stulz (2004) state that a high deal size can also be associated with hubris or agency problems. To control for the influence of transaction size, we include deal size as an log measure in the cross-sectional regression. Second, we examine the impact of cross-border transactions, as internationalization is one of the key trends in machinery manufacturing. Chatterjee et al. (1992) find an inverse relationship between perceptions of cultural differences and shareholder gains. Denis, Denis, and Yost

(2002) argue that this cultural distance should induce higher costs for post-merger integration. In contrast, Morosini, Shane and Singh (1998) find that the access to the target's diverse set of routines embedded in different cultures has a positive association to acquisition performance. We include a dummy variable to account for cross-border effects in stock price reactions. Third, we consider the target's public or private legal status. Earlier research shows that equity offers for the acquisition of public targets results in lower abnormal returns while offers for the acquisition of private firms yield higher returns for bidding shareholders (Fuller, Netter, and Stegemoller 2002). In contrast, Helwege, Pirinsky, and Stulz (2007) argue that public companies imply better available information and reduce risks of integration. We include a dummy variable to account for the public/private status of the target firm.

Acquirer characteristics have direct influence on wealth creation in mergers. They show the individual performance of acquirers and may help to explain why machinery companies apply different strategies in merger situations. Furthermore, we assume that the performance of the acquirer firm is likely to be correlated to its management quality. We examine the influence of two key variables: the prior performance of the company and the market to book value (MtBV) of the acquirer. We measure the prior performance of acquirers as a buy and hold return of acquirer stocks relative to specific index returns over the estimation period (T_{-300} to T_{-50}). As specific index return serves the relevant country-specific Datastream machinery index. As additional performance measure we include the MtBV of the acquirer firm. According to literature, differences in firm's book-to-market ratios are related to differences in future expected cash-flow and earnings growth as well as future profitability (Davis, Fama, and French 2000; Cohen, Polk, and Vuolteenaho 2003). For acquiring firms a high MtBV might result in lower abnormal excess returns, as the merger might imply that lower valued targets are acquired or that risks of future cash flows increases. We include the variable for bidder firms measuring the MtBV at T_{-21}. Table 2.4 and 2.5 present descriptive statistics about the variable composition of our data set.

Table 2.4 Variable definition and source description

This table contains the definitions and data sources for each applied variable to the character of industry characteristics, deal characteristics, and acquirer characteristics.

Variable name	Definition	Source
Industry characteristics		
Industry concentration	Measure of industry concentration using the sales based Herfindahl-Hirschman index (HHI).	Thomson One Banker (Public/Private Comp.)
Industry growth	Cumulative average growth rate (CAGR) three years before the merger announcement.	Thomson One Banker (Public Company)
Acquirer/rival CAR	Cumulative abnormal return of acquirer or rival returns for selected observation windows.	Event study results (market model)
Deal characteristics		
Log Transaction size	Natural logarithm of the transaction volume of the merger.	Thomson One Banker
Cross-border	Dummy variable if target and acquirer have different home countries.	Thomson One Banker
Target public/ private status	Dummy variable if the target company is publicly listed or in private ownership.	Thomson One Banker
Acquirer characteristics		
Prior performance	The buy and hold return of the acquirer relative to the specific stock index over the estimation period.	Datastream
MtBV acquirer	The market to book value of the acquirer measured at T_{-21}.	Thomson One Banker/Datastream

Table 2.5 Descriptive statistics on continuous and binary variables

This table describes the data collected for the description of industry characteristics, deal characteristics, and acquirer characteristics. Proportions are reported for binary variables. Mean, median, standard deviation, minimum, and maximum are reported for continuous variables.

Variable name	N	Proportion	Mean	Median	Stdev.	Minimum	Maximum
Industry characteristics							
Ind. concentr. high	64	19.4%	-	-	-	-	-
Ind. concentr. low	266	80.6%	-	-	-	-	-
Industry growth	330	-	-4.3%	-4.2%	3.4%	-17.4%	12.8%
Deal characteristics							
Transaction size	330	-	241.4	68.2	903.8	20.0	14,051.7
Cross-border	144	43.6%	-	-	-	-	-
National	186	56.4%	-	-	-	-	-
Target public	58	17.6%	-	-	-	-	-
Target private	272	82.4%	-	-	-	-	-
Acquirer characteristics							
Prior Performance	309	-	5.6%	-1.0%	59.5%	-94.4%	614.4%
MtBV	318	-	2.56	2.14	6.32	0.06	66.90

2.4 Empirical results

2.4.1 Univariate analysis

Table 2.6 shows the abnormal stock returns for the full sample of machinery mergers. We find that significant wealth gains accrue to both shareholders of target and bidding firms. We observe statistically significant results for all of our six event windows with target gains between 17.4 percent and 21.2 percent while acquirer's profits range between 1.7 percent and 2.3 percent. This finding supports our assumption that mergers in the machinery industry are not motivated by management hubris or agency problems, but to create value for their shareholders. This is confirmed when we examine the correlation between the cumulative average abnormal returns between acquirer and bidder. We observe no evidence for possible wealth transfers between target and bidder shareholders (Berkovitch and Narayanan 1993).[12] An illustration of the dynamic development of abnormal returns is shown in figure 2.1.

Table 2.6 Excess stock returns to machinery manufacturers

This table shows the cumulative average abnormal return for the total sample of 330 mergers in the machinery industry during 1997-2007 for six different event windows. Statistical significance at the 1%, 5%, and 10% level is denoted with ***, **, and * respectively. The statistical significance is tested using the test-statistics of Boehmer, Musumeci, and Poulsen (1991) (z-statistic).

Event	Target (N = 58)		Acquir. (N = 309)		CWE (N = 56)		Rivals (N = 287)	
window	CAAR	z-statist.	CAAR	z-statist.	CAAR	z-statist.	CAAR	z-statist.
[-1/+1]	17.43%	7.17***	1.67%	4.65***	2.84%	2.67**	-0.12%	-0.63
[-3+1]	19.15%	7.42***	1.91%	5.06***	2.78%	2.38**	0.08%	0.47
[-3/+3]	19.08%	6.95***	1.96%	5.54***	2.51%	2.47**	0.02%	0.48
[-5+1]	20.74%	6.60***	2.21%	5.16***	3.71%	2.73***	0.18%	0.58
[-5/+5]	20.50%	6.13***	2.28%	4.23***	3.50%	2.35**	0.10%	0.50
[-10/+10]	21.21%	6.83***	1.76%	2.94***	3.35%	2.15**	0.91%	1.96*

[12] Correlation factor between target and acquirer abnormal returns amounts to 0.14 in the [-1;1] event window.

Figure 2.1 Short-term cumulative average abnormal returns

This figure shows the cumulative abnormal returns around the announcement date over the period from T-10 to T+10 for acquirer, target, combined entity, and rivals firms. Combined entity returns are calculated as the sum of the value weighted returns of target and bidder based on the market capitalization at T-21. The rival portfolio is composed of a weighted firm portfolio in the four digit SIC code where acquirer and bidder overlap.

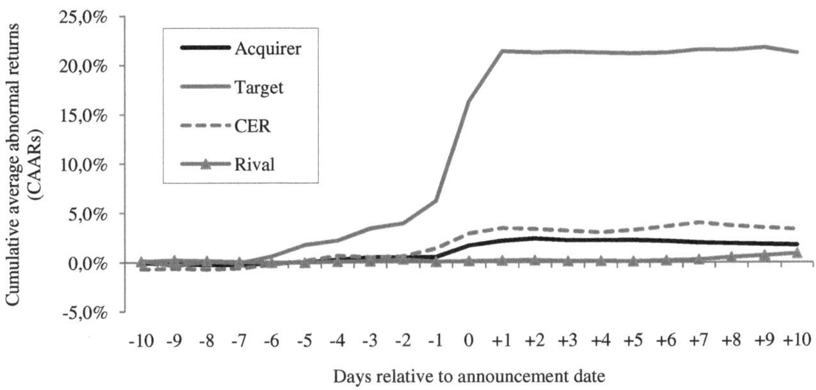

To test our hypotheses on the influence of merger motives, we perform a subsample analysis (panel A table 2.7) observing abnormal returns in the [-1;+1] event window around the announcement date.[13] Capital market reactions of transactions in fragmented and highly concentrated industries indicate a general positive abnormal announcement return for target, acquirer, and combined entity shareholders. Findings show that acquirer and target excess returns are not significantly different in concentrated or fragmented industries. Moreover, against the recent findings of Shan and Wilson (2007), specific takeover premiums for targets do not seem related to the level of industry concentration. As acquirer and target abnormal returns are not dependent on prevailing industry concentration and there are no indications for hubris

[13] Analyses for different event windows yield similar results.

and/or agency motives, results confirm our first hypothesis. Furthermore, our results contradict recent research that firm performance is negatively correlated to industry concentration (Hou and Robinson 2006), at least in the case of merger situations this finding cannot be confirmed.

The interpretation of rival reactions shows differentiated results. In panel B of table 2.7 we compare several subsamples of rival returns for concentrated and fragmented industries for the [-1;+1] event window based on different cut-off points of HHI-concentration measures. For concentrated industries, statistically significant negative rival reactions of up to -0.73 percent CAR are observed (HHI > 19.5 percent), an indication that no competitive collusion motive prevails, as otherwise positive market signaling would be evident (Eckbo 1983). In contrast, fragmented industries do not show a clear direction for rival returns with abnormal returns around zero. Testing the statistical difference of the two sample means (independent sample t-test), we find that capital market reactions are statistically different for various cut-off points of concentration (panel B). This is true for four out of seven subsamples. The rejection of monopolistic collusion motives is further strengthened if we analyze the correlation of acquirer CARs and the change in industry concentration (panel C table 2.7).

Examining the correlation between acquirer abnormal returns and change in industry concentration for various event windows and subsamples of industry concentration, we observe a negative correlation factor of -0.34 percent in the [-1;+1] event window for concentrated industries. As suggested by Ghosh (2004), we interpret this as an additional evidence to reject monopolistic collusion motives for concentrated industries, as otherwise positive correlations should have been observed. In a reverse conclusion, our findings indicate that mergers in concentrated industries are primarily dominated by efficiency gains. This seems surprising, as it contradicts our third hypothesis that primarily monopolistic collusion motives should prevail in concentrated industries. A possible explanation for this finding may be the role of antitrust legislation that regulates anticompetitive collusion in merger situations. As a market dominating positioning in an already concentrated market seems more likely to achieve, mergers that are motivated by competitive collusion are prohibited. Our results may be a signal for the successful enforcement of antirust policies confirming findings of literature that see social benefits of antitrust challenges to price collusions, anticompetitive mergers, and market power gains (e.g. Baker 2003).

Table 2.7 Subsample analysis for concentrated/fragmented industries

Panel A shows the cumulative average abnormal return for the subsample analysis of 330 mergers in the machinery industry during 1997-2007 for subsamples of concentrated and fragmented industries (HHI >0.18). Panel B shows the independent-sample t-test, testing whether the mean of rival returns for concentrated and fragmented industries statistically differs for various subsamples based on different cut-off points (HHI-concentration ratios). Panel C illustrates a correlation matrix between the change of industry concentration following a transaction and the cumulative abnormal return of the acquirer. According to Ghosh (2004), a positive correlation implies market power motives. The statistical significance is tested using the test-statistic of Boehmer, Musumeci, and Poulsen (1991) (z-statistics) and the standard t-test (t-statistics). Statistical significance at the 1%, 5%, and 10% level is denoted with ***, **, and * respectively.

Panel A: Subsample for event window [-1;+1]

	High industry concentration			Low industry concentration		
Variable name	N	CAAR	z-statist.	N	CAAR	z-statist.
Target	11	19.46%	3.82***	47	16.96%	6.10***
Acquirer	58	1.38%	2.22**	251	1.74%	4.10***
Combined Entity	11	3.90%	2.18*	45	2.58%	1.85*
Rival	55	-0.58%	-1.75*	232	-0.01%	0.01

Panel B: Mean difference test rival CARs: subsample high and low industry concentration [-1;+1]

Subsample criterion ind. concentration (HHI)	High ind. concentration			Low ind. concentration				
	N	CAR	z-stat.	N	CAR	z-stat.	Mean difference	t-stat.
0.17	62	-0.58%	-1.92*	225	0.01%	0.11	0.58%	1.653*
0.175	57	-0.58%	-1.78*	230	-0.10%	-0.58	0.57%	1.551
0.18	55	-0.58%	-1.75*	232	-0.01%	0.01	0.57%	1.518
0.185	54	-0.64%	-1.92*	233	0.00%	0.06	0.65%	1.710*
0.19	52	-0.69%	-2.01**	235	0.01%	0.08	0.69%	1.804*
0.195	48	-0.73%	-2.21**	239	0.00%	0.11	0.74%	1.843*
0.20	44	-0.58%	-1.66	243	-0.04%	-0.12	0.55%	1.314

Table 2.7 (continued)
Panel C: Correlation change of HHI and CAR acquirer

Event Window	Total	Subsample high industry concentration	Subsample low industry concentration
[-10;+10]	-4.24%	-18.40%	-2.71%
[-5;+5]	-8.56%	-19.78%	-7.06%
[-3;+3]	-6.47%	-21.19%	-4.26%
[-1;+1]	-5.50%	-33.50%	-0.19%

As results for fragmented industries (low industry concentration) are ambiguous and to specifically test our hypotheses, we divide the fragmented subsample further separating two samples with high and low change of industry concentration (see table 2.8). Similar to the results of table 2.7, we observe positive excess returns for target, acquirer, and combined entity. However, the rival return analysis yields interesting results. Analyzing rival returns for the [-1;+1] and [-3;+3] event window,[14] capital market reactions significantly differ for transactions that are accompanied by a high change of industry concentration (Δ HHI > eight percent)[15] from those that are accompanied by a low change in industry concentration (panel A table 2.8). Transactions that are accompanied by a high change of industry concentration result in significant positive rival excess returns (1.98 percent in the [-3;+3] event windows at a five percent statistical level), confirming assumptions and prerequisites of the competitive collusion hypothesis (compare table 2.1). Transactions with low change of industry concentration show unclear or negative rival reactions around the announcement date supporting evidence for productive efficiency motives.

Panel B illustrates the statistical difference test of the two samples comparing results for various definitions of high change of industry concentration (panel B). It becomes apparent that rival reactions statistically differ for various cut-off points from six percent to ten percent change of HHI indicating that in fragmented industries with

[14] Analyses for different event windows yield similar results.
[15] We test for high change of industry concentration also on a six percent and ten percent level.

strong change of industry concentration monopolistic collusion motives prevail. This evidence is further strengthened when we compare the correlation of forty transactions with highest change in industry concentration with acquirer abnormal returns in fragmented industries.[16] We observe a positive correlation of up to 41 percent in the [-10;+10] event window. According to Gosh (2004), a finding in line with competitive collusion motives. Consequently, the results only partially confirm the hypotheses we outline about merger motives in fragmented industries. Apparently both, competitive collusion and productive efficiency motives, exist in fragmented industries. However, competitive collusion motives prevail only when a high change in market concentration can be observed.

Table 2.8 Subsample analysis for fragmented industries: high/low change HHI

Panel A shows further subsample analysis for fragmented industries with high change of industry concentration (HHI) versus low change of industry concentration (HHI). In panel B we test whether the two subsamples of rival returns for strong and low change of industry concentration statistically differ for subsamples based on different cut-off points (change of HHI). Panel C illustrates a correlation matrix between change of industry concentration following a transaction and cumulative abnormal return of the acquirer. The statistical significance is tested using the test-statistic of Boehmer, Musumeci, and Poulsen (1991) (z-statistics) and the standard t-test (t-statistics). Statistical significance at the 1%, 5%, and 10% level is denoted with ***, **, and * respectively.

Panel A: Subsample fragmented industries with high/low change of industry concentration (HHI)

	High Change HHI (> 8%)			Low Change HHI (< 8%)		
	N	CAAR	z-stat.	N	CAAR	z-stat.
Event Window [-1;+1]						
Target	8	13.51%	2.77**	35	16.12%	4.78***
Acquirer	39	0.80%	0.82	182	1.78%	3.44***
Combined Entity	8	1.97%	2.09*	34	3.00%	1.56
Rival	34	0.91%[a]	1.62	169	-0.19%[a]	-0.85
Event Window [-3;+3]						
Target	8	14.05%	2.79**	35	17.39%	4.35***
Acquirer	39	0.22%	0.27	182	2.31%	4.57***
Combined Entity	8	3.03%	3.40**	34	1.70%	0.83
Rival	34	1.98%[b]	3.05***	169	-0.22%[b]	-0.27

Statistical difference between two sample means is denoted with a at the 10% level and b at the 5% level.

[16] Correlation analysis with a varying number of transactions with high change of industry concentration provide similar results.

Table 2.8 (continued)
Panel B: Mean difference test rival CARs: fragmented industries with high/low change of HHI

Subsample criterion change ind. concentration	High change HHI			Low change HHI				
	N	CAR	z-stat.	N	CAR	z-stat.	Mean difference	t-stat.
Event Window [-1;+1]								
6%	58	0.42%	0.91	145	-0.17%	-0.60	0.59%	1.243
8%	34	0.91%	1.62	169	-0.19%	-0.85	1.10%	1.791*
10%	29	0.50%	1.04	174	-0.09%	-0.38	0.58%	1.077
Event Window [-3;+3]								
6%	58	1.32%	2.75***	145	-0.31%	-0.54	1.63%	2.02**
8%	34	1.98%	3.05***	169	-0.22%	-0.27	2.18%	2.35**
10%	29	1.80%	2.69**	174	-0.12%	-0.00	1.92%	2.08**

Panel C: Correlation change of HHI and CAR acquirer (40 mergers with highest change of HHI)

Event Window	Total	Subsample high change of industry concentration	Subsample low change of industry concentration
[-10;+10]	-2.71%	40.53%	-2.67%
[-5;+5]	-7.06%	22.92%	-8.01%
[-3;+3]	-4.26%	30.91%	-4.67%
[-1;+1]	-0.19%	29.61%	-1.28%

Correlation results for different subsample sizes (30-50 transactions) yield similar results with positive correlation between change of HHI and CAR acquirer.

In summary, our initial hypothesis that industry concentration influences merger motives of the management finds empirical support. While in highly concentrated industries no indication for competitive collusions exists, in fragmented industries we identify both competitive collusion and productive efficiency motives. To strengthen observations of the univariate analysis and to filter dilution effects, we jointly examine defined industry characteristics, deal characteristics, and acquirer characteristics and conduct a multivariate analysis in the following section.

2.4.2 *Cross-sectional regression analysis*

By comparing wealth mechanics of target, acquirer, and rival firms for fragmented and concentrated industries, we gain further evidence if industry concentration influences merger motives. We perform multivariate analyses of defined variables to jointly measure the effect on shareholder value using cumulative abnormal returns over the [-1;+1], the [-5;+1], and the [-10;+10] event windows as dependent variable.[17] We conduct two models in cross-section. In the first model, we analyze wealth determinants for the whole sample of acquirer and rival returns to measure the overall impact of industry concentration on stock returns. In the second model, we perform cross-section analysis for two subsamples of fragmented and concentrated industries. By comparing the differences in wealth mechanics we are able to illuminate and extend relationships among industry concentration and merger motives. The results are shown in table 2.9 and 2.10. We compute all test statistics using White's (1980) heteroskedasticity-consistent covariance matrix.

Analyzing acquirer wealth mechanics across different event windows (table 2.9), we observe the impact of industry characteristics and acquirer variables on abnormal return creation. Underlying industry concentration seems to have a significant negative influence on overall wealth creation confirming an influence on the magnitude of acquirer returns. This finding is in line with Clelland, Douglas, and Henderson (2006) who observe a moderating effect of industry concentration on the relationship between competitive value and competitive advantage. However, the result contradicts our first hypothesis, although results are only statistically significant in the [-1;+1] event window. The variable rival excess returns inversely influences acquirer returns. Although this finding does not imply a cause-effect relationship, it shows that excess returns of acquirer and rival firms are mutually interlinked. Considering value maximizing behavior of firms, management should carefully consider possible impact on overall industry environment.

---

[17] An analysis of cumulative abnormal returns for different event windows yields similar returns.

The defined deal variables do not show significant influence on overall wealth creation in mergers. Nonetheless, the inverse relationship of log transaction size with acquirer abnormal returns can possibly be explained with a size/risk effect of transaction. A larger target implies more integration risk, consequently abnormal returns are related negatively. As expected, the cross-border dummy variable shows a negative relationship reflecting a higher integration risk of transactions while the dummy variable public/private status of targets has a negative coefficient. This may support the findings of Fuller, Netter, and Stegemoller (2002) of higher abnormal returns for bidding shareholders for private companies. The acquirer variables prior performance and MtBV show both statistically significant negative influence on acquirer abnormal returns. Apparently, capital markets evaluate merger decisions of well performing acquirers lower than of worse performing acquirers. Dong et al. (2002) show that firms with higher valuations have lower announcement returns, probably because highly valued acquirers communicate to the market that these high valuations are not warranted by fundamentals, as they are undertaking efforts to acquire potentially less overvalued assets with more overvalued equity.

The acquirer cross-section analysis in model II compares the overall wealth mechanics of fragmented and concentrated industries. Results show that wealth determinants in fragmented and concentrated subsamples are partially different. Even though statistical significance is low, the coefficients are opposite for variables "CAR rival", "cross-border" and "target public/private status". CAR rival has a positive correlation for concentrated industries implying that less negative rival returns are associated with higher acquirer returns. [18] This result indicates that a relative improvement of rival positioning in the market positively affects acquirer returns. We interpret this as another effect from antitrust legislation as a lower market impact results in less anticompetitive regulation by authorities and consequently results in increased merger rents. The variables "cross-border" and "public/private status" of the target firm show a positive, not significant coefficient in concentrated sub-industries

[18] Rival CAARs in concentrated industries are observed to be negative.

and a negative coefficient in fragmented sub-industries. While in fragmented industries an internationalization strategy may be connected to additional integration risks, in concentrated markets cross-border transactions may be acknowledged by capital markets as possible means to enter new markets and to expand global presence. In less consolidated industries the acquisition of a private company is seen more advantageous, possibly indicating a size effect of transaction (Moeller, Schlingemann, and Stulz 2004).

Table 2.9 Multivariate analysis of acquirer abnormal returns

This table shows estimation results for OLS regression models with acquirer cumulative abnormal returns as dependent variable for three different event windows. We test the influence of industry characteristics to measure the impact on merger motives as well as defined deal and acquirer characteristics. The test statistic is computed using White's (1980) heteroskedasticity-consistent covariance matrix. Statistical significance at the 1%, 5%, and 10% level is denoted with ***, **, and * respectively.

Variable name	Model I: Acquirer CAAR			Model II: subsample Acquirer CAAR [-1;+1]	
	CAAR [-1;+1]	CAAR [-5;+1]	CAAR [-10;+10]	fragmented (HHI < 0.18)	concentrated (HHI > 0.18)
Intercept	0.018	0.048	0.059	0.016	-0.009
	0.808	*1.675**	*1.450*	*0.654*	*-0.246*
Industry characteristics					
Ind. concentration	-0.090	-0.032	-0.111	-	-
	*-1.765**	*-0.559*	*-1.330*	-	-
CAGR industry	-0.101	-0.101	-0.115	-0.066	-0.325
	-0.886	*-0.674*	*-0.691*	*-0.546*	*-0.767*
CAR rival	-0.221	-0.216	-0.195	-0.249	0.069
	-1.294	*-1.889**	*-1.743**	*-1.270*	*0.280*
Deal variables					
Log deal size	0.007	-0.008	-0.011	0.006	0.002
	0.709	*-0.704*	*-0.693*	*0.529*	*0.130*
Cross-border	-0.007	-0.014	-0.008	-0.010	0.009
	-0.798	*-1.408*	*-0.573*	*-1.066*	*0.567*
Target public/ private	-0.016	-0.014	-0.019	-0.021	0.011
	-1.473	*-0.973*	*-1.179*	*-1.683**	*0.615*
Acquirer variables					
Prior perform.	-0.020	-0.039	-0.052	-0.021	-0.011
	*-3.246****	*-4.621****	*-3.819****	*-3.504****	*-0.274*
MtBV acquirer	-0.001	-0.001	-0.001	-0.002	-0.001
	*-2.732****	*-1.942**	*-0.943*	*-1.083*	*-3.220****
N	262	262	262	214	48
Adj. R squared	0.029	0.058	0.060	0.025	-0.095

The main finding of the cross-section analysis of rival firms (table 2.10) is that wealth mechanics vary drastically for industries with different industry concentration backgrounds. A first indication is the statistically negative influence of the variable "industry concentration" in model I. The higher the industry concentration, the more negatively rival companies react. In line with the univariate analysis, this rejects monopolistic motives in concentrated industries. Besides this finding, we again confirm the mutual negative correlation of rival CARs and acquirer CARs. The defined deal characteristics seem not to directly determine abnormal return developments of rivals, as we observe no statistically significant relationships. This is different with the variables of acquirer characteristics that show statistically significant negative coefficients. We interpret this as signal to the market that well performing acquirers are more likely to realize higher efficiency improvements and/or market power gains than poor performing acquirers leading to a more negative impact for rival shareholders. Further splitting the analysis in subsamples of fragmented and concentrated industries (model II), results indicate that cause and effect relationships are substantially different. Nearly all defined variables (with the exception of the CAGR industry growth) show opposite coefficients for mergers in concentrated and fragmented industries. Besides their low statistical significance, we conclude that wealth mechanics of rival companies are virtually opposite. Apparently, the impact on competition (rival reactions) varies for companies with different industry concentration backgrounds pointing to different underlying merger motives in concentrated and fragmented industries.

In conclusion, we show in cross-sectional regression that wealth creation mechanisms are different especially for rival companies in dependence of the prevailing degree of industry concentration (nearly all variables show opposite coefficients). Considering value maximizing behavior of managers in an equilibrium of competition, this should lead to different merger motives in M&A situations. Furthermore, the findings confirm univariate results regarding underlying merger motives in concentrated and fragmented industries. We find evidence for the absence of monopolistic collusion motives in concentrated industries.

Table 2.10 Multivariate analysis of rival abnormal returns

This table shows estimation results for OLS regression models with rival cumulative abnormal returns as dependent variable in the [-1;+1] event window. We test the influence of industry characteristics to measure the impact on merger motives as well as defined deal and acquirer characteristics. The test statistic is computed using White's (1980) heteroskedasticity-consistent covariance matrix. Statistical significance at the 1%, 5%, and 10% level is denoted with ***, **, and * respectively.

Variable name	Model I: Rival CAAR			Model II: Subsample Rival CAAR [-1;+1]	
	CAAR [-1;+1]	CAAR [-5;+1]	CAAR [-10;+10]	fragmented (HHI < 0.18)	concentrated (HHI > 0.18)
Intercept	0.004	0.007	0.039	0.005	-0.038
	0.528	*0.473*	*1.317*	*0.620*	*-2.754****
Industry characteristics					
Ind. concentration	-0.034	-0.035	-0.040	-	-
	*-1.652**	*-1.164*	*-0.666*	-	-
CAGR industry	-0.063	-0.172	-0.221	-0.047	-0.175
	-0.918	*-1.491*	*-1.059*	*-0.628*	*-1.175*
CAR acquirer	*-0.036*	-0.061	*-0.127*	-0.038	0.014
	-1.598	*-2.297***	*-1.665**	*-1.601*	*0.289*
Deal variables					
Log deal size	-0.001	-0.002	-0.013	-0.004	0.013
	-0.261	*-0.339*	*-1.140*	*-0.945*	*1.879**
Cross-border	-0.003	-0.002	0.009	-0.005	0.004
	-0.861	*-0.294*	*0.725*	*-1.084*	*0.575*
Target public/ private	-0.002	-0.010	-0.009	0.001	-0.013
	-0.348	*-1.321*	*-0.654*	*0.204*	*-1.491*
Acquirer variables					
Prior perform.	*-0.003*	-0.008	*0.014*	-0.003	0.004
	-1.485	*-1.910**	*2.051***	*-1.790**	*0.448*
MtBV acquirer	*-0.000*	*-0.001*	*-0.001*	0.001	-0.001
	-0.852	*-1.861**	*-1.929**	*0.777*	*-3.514****
N	262	262	262	214	48
Adj. R squared	-0.002	0.019	0.021	-0.003	0.000

2.5 Summary and conclusion

The objective of this study is to examine the impact of industry concentration on merger motives of companies. We follow the argumentation of industrial organization theory and argue that exogenous market factors (e.g. industry concentration) determine endogenous market conduct (industry motives). As a direct parameterization is difficult, we follow recommendation of literature and investigate share price reactions to merger announcements to identify underlying merger motives. To gain further reliability of results, we combine event study methodology with an approach of Gosh (2004) and additionally examine the correlation of acquirer returns and the change in industry concentration to differentiate collusion motives. The analysis concentrates on a sample of 330 transactions in the machinery industry between 1997 and 2007. We limit ourselves to machinery transactions because of unique market characteristics such as homogeneity of general market trends and heterogeneity of industry concentration in submarkets. By linking academic research of merger motives and industrial organization theory, we derive our research hypothesis.

We conduct univariate analysis, multivariate regression, and correlation analysis and gain valuable insights into determinants of merger motives. First, we observe that rival excess returns are significantly different in subsamples of concentrated and fragmented industries. In contrast, acquirer and target abnormal returns do not show significant divergence for different degrees of industry concentration. Together with a negative correlation of acquirer excess returns and change of industry concentration, we conclude that competitive collusion is not a major motive for firms in concentrated industries and that those mergers are driven primarily by productive efficiency gains. Second, in fragmented industries we detect different rival reactions in subsamples of industries with high and low change of industry concentration. Against the background of academic literature and in combination with correlation analysis, we find evidence that in fragmented industries both, collusion and productive efficiency, are prevailing motives of firm mergers. The results are confirmed by cross-sectional regression highlighting a substantial difference in wealth creation mechanics for fragmented and concentrated industries. Assuming value maximizing behavior of management, those differences should finally lead to different merger motives of management depending on their underlying level of industry concentration.

In conclusion, our results provide additional perspectives on the empirical analysis of research motives behind mergers. Against most empirical research (e.g. Trautwein 1990; Fee and Thomas 2004; Ghosh 2004), we find support for monopolistic collusion motives in mergers that result in significant wealth creation for the transaction partners. Our analysis provides explanations why broader empirical studies fail to identify monopolistic motives. First, in concentrated industries monopolistic collusion seems successfully impeded by antitrust legislation. Second, in fragmented industries only a limited number of merger transactions is able to realize significant market power gains. If this general market background is not considered in empirical analysis, monopolistic collusion motives are difficult to identify. We assume that the analysis of merger motives will gain additional refinement if the influence of market characteristics such as industry concentration are considered.

3 Corporate Relatedness and Wealth Creation in Machinery Mergers

3.1 Introduction

Corporate vertical integration and diversification strategies are fundamental topics in strategic management research. Despite an increasing recognition of the role of relatedness for wealth creation in mergers (Maksimovic and Philipps 2001; Fan and Goyal 2006), recent empirical studies (Graham, Lemmon, and Wolf 2002; Villalonga 2004) and business consulting literature (McKinsey 2004; RBSC 2005; PWC 2008) challenge the long predominating view that multi-business firms are inefficient and refresh discussion on the appropriate corporate focus of firms. We shed additional light on this discussion providing an industry-specific analysis of merger decisions of firms for various degrees of relatedness.

Motives and potential benefits of corporate focus and diversification strategies in mergers are well entrenched in theoretical considerations. Researchers argue that value creation in related acquisitions is mostly associated with economic efficiencies arising from economies of scale and scope, from operating efficiencies, and from market power (Rumelt 1974; Seth 1990; Walker 2000). Similarly, vertical integration allows firms to circumvent contractual inefficiencies, allocate residual rights of control, increase market power, or foster collusive behavior (Stigler 1964; Trautwein 1990; Walker 2000; Shahrur 2005). On the other hand, diversifying transactions allow rent-seeking firms to diversify in response to excess capacity in their productive factors (Montgomery 1994) and can enable mature, slow-growing firms to explore new attractive markets (Gomes and Livdan 2004). Empirical research seems to agree that the right corporate focus contributes to wealth generation in mergers (Brunner 2002) and that diversified companies trade at a discount (Lang and Stulz 1994; Servaes 1996; Denis, Denis, and Yost 2002). However, there is growing criticism that interprets empirically tested differences between conglomerate and specialized firm performance as sample selection effects (Campa and Kedia 2002; Gomes and Livdan 2004) and/or methodological relatedness classification effects (Fan and Goyal 2006). Furthermore, most empirical studies on relatedness often do not adequately account for different industry logics and drivers (Fowler and Schmidt 1988; Mitchell and Mulherin 1996). Fan and Goyal (2006) summarize that there is little knowledge about relatedness implications in mergers for particular industries.

To overcome methodological shortcomings of cross-industry studies and to meet practitioners demand, we analyze relatedness implications for mergers in the machinery industry. We concentrate on this industry because of its heterogeneous business strategies of market participants (conglomerates versus specialized business firms) which allows to adequately scrutinize different merger decisions. One recent example is KUKA, operating in areas of packaging machinery, textile engineering, control technology, forming, and machine tools until 2007. Today, it is a focused market leader in robotics manufacturing and automation, as management decided to reduce business complexity because there are "no strategic, operational, or financial advantages to retaining other divisions" (Kuka 2007). Major rivals of KUKA decided for the opposite strategy engaging in diversifying mergers (e.g. Johnson Controls, Kawasaki Heavy Industries, Hitachi). We seek to generate an understanding of how capital markets evaluate such merger decisions and the relevance of relationship and industry interaction between acquirer and target firm (relatedness). To identify dominant logics of machinery mergers, we base our analysis on 330 transactions between 1997 and 2007 examining target, acquirer, and rival reactions in different contexts of corporate relatedness. To account for the complexity of relatedness classification in empirical studies, we use commodity flow data to construct quantitative measures of relatedness (Fan and Lang 2000; Fan and Goyal 2006). With the input-output (IO) data, we capture the relation between a pair of merging firms from the dollar amount of input transfer between the industries in which the merging firms operate.

Our results confirm findings of existing research that the right corporate focus is value contributing in mergers, as relatedness is a major determinant of wealth. As expected, horizontal mergers show highest value creation for acquirer shareholders and the combined entity attributed to theoretical benefits such as economies of scale and scope, operating efficiencies, and market power (Rumelt 1974; Seth 1990; Walker 2000). The differences in acquirer returns of related and diversifying transactions are significant. We find surprising results for vertical/complementary transactions, as the direction of the takeover is important. Vertical downstream mergers (backward integration), primarily associated with securing a stable supply of inputs and quality of products, do not show significant value creation for shareholders while vertical upstream mergers (forward integration) show similar positive wealth effects as horizontal mergers. Forward integration provides significant potential for machinery firms to control subsequent stages of production, to influence sales markets, and to improve their product or service offering. This result suggests that the discussion on the right corporate focus needs to include value chain considerations of firms. Furthermore, we observe positive average wealth effects to acquirer and combined entity firms in unrelated transactions rejecting findings that diversification destroys value. We find that additional wealth determinants significantly influence the value potential of transactions including target characteristics as well as acquirer's internal capacities and experiences to manage pre- and post-merger transactions. Eventually, also the individual situation of target and acquirer firms accounts for a large proportion of wealth generation in mergers.

The remainder of the paper is structured as follows. In section 3.2 we review current literature focusing on theoretical and empirical findings regarding relatedness between target and acquirer. After a description of major machinery industry trends, we derive our hypotheses. In section 3.3, we explain the method of measuring relatedness, discuss our econometric model, give descriptive statistics on the data sample, and identify cross-sectional factors that potentially determine wealth creation. In section 3.4, we conduct both univariate and multivariate analysis to identify the influence of relatedness on merger success. We conclude with a discussion of findings (section 3.5).

3.2 Literature review, market characteristics, and hypothesis development

3.2.1 Literature review on relatedness

Research on relatedness often concentrates on motivations and implications associated with certain types of relatedness. It usually separates in horizontal, vertical, complementary, and diversifying types of transactions.

Theoretical considerations focusing on horizontal transactions relate primarily to efficiency, collusion, or hubris/agency motives of acquiring firms. The efficiency view highlights incentives of firms to engage in horizontal mergers in order to realize cost or revenue synergies (Rumelt 1974; Walker 2000). In contrast, the monopolistic collusion theory postulates that horizontal takeovers are attempts by merging firms to facilitate collusion in order to expropriate wealth from customers and suppliers (Stigler 1964; Sharur 2005). Further research on horizontal mergers focuses on explaining why mergers sometimes destroy wealth for bidding shareholders (hubris/agency theories). Empirical studies show that at least parts of sometimes large share price increases of target firms are attributed to a general wealth transfer from bidder to target (Walking and Long 1984; Roll 1986; Seyhun 1990). Besides hubris or agency problems, most empirical studies confirm horizontal relatedness to be value enhancing in mergers, as efficiency and market power considerations persist (Brunner 2002).

Vertical mergers provide acquiring firms with ownership and control over adjacent stages of the production process and/or allow firms to substitute internal exchanges within boundaries of the firm for contractual or market exchanges (Fan and Goyal 2006; Lafontaine and Slade 2007). A prominent view why firms merge vertically is based on the transaction cost theory that sees vertical integration as a way of circumventing contractual inefficiencies, when costs of using markets exceed costs of internal organization (Coase 1937; Williamson 1979; Crocker 1983). Another theory links vertical mergers to ownership of assets as a way of allocating residual rights of control in response to incomplete contracting (Grossman and Hart 1986; Hart and Moore 1990; Ordover, Saloner, and Salop 1990). Fontenay and Gans (2005) demonstrate that vertical integration can alter the joint payoff of integrating parties in ex-post bargaining. An integrated firm will recognize that it can benefit from higher costs imposed on its downstream rivals when it refrains from aggressive pricing in input markets (Salinger 1988; Ordover, Saloner, and Salop 1990). This aspect refers to better coordination, since rivals need access to input (output) being controlled by the integrated entity (Chen 2001; Nocke and White 2007). Empirical work also confirms the importance of the direction of integration. Lafontaine and Slade (2007) summarize that firm's decisions to integrate forward often relies on incentive and moral-hazard type arguments, whereas the empirical literature on backward integration mostly tests predictions derived from transaction-cost theory.

If acquirer and target company have a large overlap in adjacent stages of their value chain, e.g. similar sourcing markets (backward complementarity) or similar sales markets (forward complementarity), a merger is classified as complementary. Potential advantages behind complementary transactions are, for example, benefits of the acquirer from strong sales or distribution networks of targets as well as efficiency effects in sourcing activities. A higher segmental complementarity implies greater similarity in procurement and marketing activities and may therefore enhance the economy-of-scale effect of complementary mergers (Fan and Lang 2000). Although empirical examination of the complementarity of target and acquirer is scarce, wealth creation should be positive in the case of a complementary merger and induce higher wealth gains than unrelated mergers.

Although theories on diversification are a thoroughly investigated area of research, empirical evidence remains ambiguous. Recent research provides evidence to positive effects of corporate diversification (Graham, Lemmon, and Wolf 2002; Villalonga 2004) through advantages of economies of scope, elimination of redundancies across different activities, lower fix costs of production, and new market opportunities (Gomes and Livdan 2004). Furthermore, unrelated transactions are sometimes attributed to a coinsurance effect (if cash flows of combined firms are not perfectly correlated, the maximum leverage increases after acquisition) and a diversification of risk (Amihud and Lev 1981; Seth 1990). Besides these theoretical benefits, performance studies in particular show that conglomerates trade at a discount relative to a portfolio of comparable standalone firms (Lang and Stulz 1994; Servaes 1996; Denis, Denis, and Yost 2002). Explanations for this "diversification discount" have generally emphasized agency and behavioral problems (Denis, Denis, and Sarin 1997; Hyland and Diltz 2002), but also include other considerations as, for example, national differences in corporate governance (Lins and Servaes 1999).

Concluding, prior research suggests that presence and type of relatedness are important factors for explaining and determining wealth effects in merger situations. Based on above literature, we discuss major machinery-specific market characteristics and trends to derive our research hypotheses refining suggestions of literature review with regard to wealth creation in machinery mergers. The following section therefore provides a general industry overview as well as a discussion of major trends in the machinery industry.

3.2.2 Market characteristics of the machinery industry

The machinery industry is a complex environment with major heterogeneity in its product offerings and market structures. With an estimated global market volume of approximately USD 1,850bn in 2007, the machinery industry accounts for a high proportion of economic outputs and plays an important role as driver of global development through innovations and technological advancements (Bureau of Economic Analysis 2008; VDMA 2008). Following a general segmentation, the machinery industry can be divided into two primary segments: "Special purpose machinery" produces machinery for industries along the categories farm machinery and garden equipment, construction machinery & mining equipment, and special industry machinery equipment. The second segment "general purpose machinery" includes machinery without specific industry focus and industrial components: refrigeration and heating equipment, metalworking machinery, engine and turbine equipment, and other general purpose machinery (US Department of Labor 2007). The biggest market for global machinery are the Americas with 38 percent market share, followed by the Asia-Pacific region with 31 percent. Europe accounts for 28 percent of global machinery revenues (Datamonitor 2009).[19]

Although machinery manufacturers are a heterogeneous compound of branches and sub-industries, there are several general trends with an overall influence on market developments and strategic behaviors of machinery market participants.[20] First, the emergence of strong competition in emerging economies changes the overall market environment. Low cost competitors are putting increasing pressure on Western markets and premium segments, as price levels are set by globally sourcing customers. At the same time, regional sales markets are shifting because of the growing importance of emerging markets in Asia and Eastern Europe. Machinery manufacturers have to respond to this ongoing globalization by adapting to international production price levels, by gaining access to growth markets, and by developing global footprint designs.

Second, the strong competition and the cost pressure from customers (who pass on their own cost pressure) increase the need for operational excellence and efficiency improvements. In this context, a sophisticated management of value chain might include increasing vertical integration to ensure stable profitability levels and competitive advantages. Production skills often serve as unique selling proposition among competing firms. To sustain the positioning of the firm, a fast pace in innovation and technological development is required. As product differentiation via price level becomes increasingly difficult, product innovation, e.g. process control technology and steering software, gains growing importance in production and development processes of machinery manufacturers.

---

[19] Global market share information is based on a market definition of Datastream (2009).

[20] Deloitte (2003; 2006), CME (2004), RBSC and VDMA (2007) provide comprehensive descriptions of major machinery industry trends.

Third, changing client requirements intensify the above described trends. Clients increasingly demand tailored solutions for their specific situation resulting in an increase of complexity in production processes. To meet reliably and cost effectively customer requirements, standardization (e.g. modularization), automatization, and flexibility in production are key success factors for machinery manufacturers. In addition, the product portfolio of machinery manufacturers continues to shift towards service offerings (e.g. after sales services or operator models) as higher margins and customer loyalty can be achieved. Consequently, machinery manufacturers increasingly develop from pure module and machine manufacturers to system and integrated solution providers. In this situation, merger & acquisitions have been discovered as suitable strategy by machinery manufacturers to cope with the developments and challenges of global markets. This is reflected in more than 5.700 M&A transactions reported globally between 1997 to 2007.

3.2.3 Hypothesis development

The above discussed industry trends and challenges should be reflected in merger decisions and motivations of machinery firms (Fowler and Schmidt 1988; Mitchell and Mulherin 1996). We believe that the general suggestion put forward by theoretical and empirical literature that related transactions imply positive wealth effects to shareholders should hold true. Related transactions are a possible way for machinery manufacturers to realize necessary efficiency improvements, cost savings in production processes (synergies), and market power effects. Consequently, we expect related transactions to return higher synergies and economies of scale/scope and thus result in more positive capital market evaluations.

H I: Corporate relatedness has positive influence on wealth generation in mergers.

In accordance to recent empirical evidence (Fan and Goyal 2006), vertical mergers should show a positive capital market evaluation highlighting benefits such as circumvention of contractual inefficiencies, residual rights of control, and/or an increase in market power. In line with literature and market trends, there should be some additional refinement regarding the direction of the merger. Vertical upstream mergers may facilitate control and access to subsequent stages of production as well as a better synchronization of supply and demand. Consequently, internal complexity of production processes can possibly be reduced through standardization and greater flexibility. Furthermore, vertical upstream mergers may also improve the service portfolio provided to customers (e.g. after-sales services, operator models) and thus allow for better meeting market demands (integrated service offering). In contrast, the advantages from backward integration (make or buy decision) to secure a stable supply of inputs and to ensure a consistent quality of the product may be limited. While advantages and potential positive effects of vertical upstream integration should outweigh the increased complexity of an integrated value chain, this potential should not, or to a lesser extent, be present in vertical backward oriented industries. We propose a similar argument for complementary transactions, as the influence on upstream markets allows firms to improve strategic positioning, as cross-selling or additional services provide a suitable basis for business development of target and acquirer firm.

H II: For vertical and complementary transactions, the direction of the integration will influence wealth generation in mergers.

Against the background of saturated markets in the machinery industry, diversifying transactions are possible means to enter new markets and to engage in different business segments. In the highly competitive market environment of machinery manufacturers these advantages of diversification decisions should generate positive excess returns in merger situations. Considering the strong increase in complexity required to handle additional production processes and client demands, we hypothesize that abnormal returns should be lowest for unrelated transactions.

H III: Though diversification should be least appreciated by capital markets, we expect a general positive influence on abnormal returns.

3.3 Data and methodology

3.3.1 Sample composition

Our sample includes mergers and acquisitions from the Thomson One Banker deal database announced globally between January 1, 1997 and December 31, 2007. For our analysis we include all transactions that fulfill the following requirements:

(1) The acquirer is a machinery manufacturer and has sufficient stock information available.
(2) The transaction is a majority investment (>50 percent share after deal completion).
(3) The deal value is at least USD 20 million.
(4) Transactions by one acquirer do not overlap within the estimation period of 250 days.
(5) The acquirer's primary SIC code is not part of computer equipment and office machines.
(6) Transaction details are confirmed by Factiva press research.

Between 1997 and 2007 more than 5.700 M&A transactions are reported for the machinery industry. For the purpose of this study, several selection criteria are applied to refine the sample. By applying criterion (1), we include only transactions where sufficient stock market data is available to estimate abnormal returns via the market model. Criterion (2) and (3) ensure that the impact of the transaction of both acquirer and target company is above a specified minimum threshold, in order to assure that merger motives are sufficiently reflected in deal participant's and rival's share price reactions. To maximize the reliability of our data sample, we exclude transactions with overlapping M&A transactions in the observation period (criterion 4). To focus on machinery manufacturers only, we exclude all companies under the SIC classification computer manufacturing (criterion 5).[21] We confirm each of the remaining transactions by screening news articles from the Factiva database for misspecification (criterion 6). Applying criteria (1) to (6) we yield a total sample of 330 transactions.

To examine the merger impact on industry and competition, we study rival reactions identifying 880 relevant rival firms from Thomson One Banker Peer Analysis database. In our analysis, we consider as rivals any company (besides the bidder and target) that reports its primary four-digit SIC code in the industry where acquirer and target overlap. If there is no overlap, we use the primary SIC code of acquirers to test for rival reactions. For our rival portfolio, we include all companies with revenues larger than USD 1 million where sufficient share data is available via Datastream. For the average deal in our sample, we identify 23 rival firms to calculate abnormal stock returns in the announcement period.

3.3.2 Calculation of announcement period abnormal returns

To answer the hypotheses generated through literature review and general market analysis, we focus on capital market reactions following merger announcements measuring the short-term impact on transaction participant's share prices and corresponding returns. Price developments of acquirer, target, combined entity, and rival companies are validated against market returns in specified time-windows determining abnormal returns to shareholders.[22] We use event study methodology in connection with a standard market model as derived by Brown and Warner (1985) and measure capital market reactions around the announcement date.

We estimate abnormal returns for firm i at date t (AR_{it}) as $AR_{it} = R_{it} - \alpha_i - \beta_i R_{mt}$, where R_{mt} is the return of a market portfolio that refers to a market index associated

[21] We excluded 3570 computer & office equipment, 3571 electronic computers, 3572 computer storage devices, 3575 computer terminals, 3576 computer communication equipment, 3577 computer peripheral equipment.

[22] Abnormal returns describe the difference between the expected return (estimated by the market model) and the actual return observed in the market.

with the given securities over time. For the purpose of this analysis, we use for each security the relevant country-specific Datastream industrial machinery index. Our market model parameters are estimated over an observation period of 250 trading days starting at day T_{-300} to T_{-50} relative to the announcement date T_0. We exclude all companies with fewer trading days available from our sample. We apply the announcement date as reported by Thomson One Banker, cross-checking the information using press research via Factiva. To obtain the cumulative abnormal return (CAR) of a transaction, we perform an ordinary leased squared (OLS) regression over six different event windows ranging between two days [-1;+1] and 20 days [-10;+10] around the announcement date. We estimate combined wealth effects (CWE) of merging companies as the cumulative abnormal return (CAR) to a value weighted portfolio of acquirer and target (Bradley, Desai, and Kim 1988). We weight the merging firms with their respective market values of equity at day T_{-21} relative to the announcement date. To estimate CARs for rival companies, we create value weighted rival portfolios (excluding acquirer and target) for the relevant primary four-digit SIC code where bidder and target overlap.

To test for statistical significance of cumulated abnormal returns, we follow Harrington and Shrider (2007) and apply test statistics of Boehmer, Musumeci, and Poulsen (1991), an enhancement of the approach by Patell (1976):

$$z = \frac{\frac{1}{N}\sum_{i=1}^{N} SR_{i,t}}{\sqrt{\frac{1}{N(N-1)}\sum_{i=1}^{N}\left(SR_{i,t} - \sum_{i=1}^{N}\frac{SR_{i,t}}{N}\right)^2}}$$

where $SR_{i,t}$ is:

$$SR_{i,t} = \frac{AR_{i,t}}{s_i\sqrt{1 + \frac{1}{T_i} + \frac{(R_{m,E} - \bar{R}_m)^2}{\sum_{t=1}^{T}(R_{m,t} - \bar{R}_M)^2}}}$$

N : Number of stocks in the sample

$AR_{i,t}$: Abnormal returns of stock i at event day t

$R_{m,t}$: Market return on day t

$\bar{R}_m$: Average market return during estimation period

s_i : The variance of the residuals during the estimation period, calculated as

$$s_i = \sqrt{\frac{1}{T-2}\sum_{t=1}^{T} AR_{i,t}^2}$$

T_i : Number of days of security i in estimation period

The test considers the likely difference in cross-sectional return variance between the estimation period from T_{-300} to T_{-50} and the event window. The test statistic z follows a student t-distribution with T-2 degrees of freedom. The test results appear to be robust also in absence of event-induced variance increases (Serra 2004).

3.3.3 Classification of relatedness

Relatedness is difficult to conceptualize, parameterize, and measure. In literature, there exist mainly three methods to measure relatedness between firms (Lien and Klein 2008): (1) subjective judgment from press research or company documents, (2) classification based on SIC codes, and (3) classification based on commodity flow data. The first approach categorizes businesses into related or unrelated using subjective classification by comparing parameters such as inputs, production technology, distribution channels, and customers between the relevant industries. If similarities can be found, relatedness between industries is assumed (Rumelt 1974). A major weakness of this approach is the subjective component in the evaluation. Reviewing every transaction in our data sample for available information we conclude that public information is scarce and does not provide a reliable source for relatedness classification.

The second approach to classify relatedness is based on SIC codes. Industries are classified as related if two industries share the same two-, three-, or four-digit SIC code. Besides its sometimes unreliable market definitions, a SIC code-based classification fails to reveal different types of relatedness. Although there exists a hierarchy within the SIC classification system, there remain difficulties in determining clear relationships especially for vertical transactions (Fan and Lang 2000). The SIC-based classification is still very popular in empirical research as it can easily be applied to large data samples. However, as we want to examine special forms of forward and backward relation and complementarity between target and acquirer, the SIC-based classification is not sufficient for a complex inter-industry analysis of relatedness.

A third approach developed by Fan and Lang (2000) captures inter-industry and inter-segment relatedness through the use of commodity flow data from input-output tables provided by the US Bureau of Economic Analysis.[23] Use tables show economic statistics about the dollar value of industry i's output required to produce industry j's total output, denoted as a_{ij}. Following this method, a judgment about relatedness between a pair of industries can be deducted. However, this approach still has some weaknesses. First, as input-output tables display US data only and our analysis focuses on worldwide machinery transactions, there exists a potential source of discrepancy. However, we believe that the relations between a pair of industries i and j should be reflected on a country-level as much as on a worldwide basis. Second, the IO approach implies the comparison of industry level data with firm specific merger performance. Expected results may allow for identifying general influence and wealth patterns of relatedness in mergers, however, firm specific implications may vary.

---

[23] "Use Tables" provided by the Bureau of Economic Analysis (US department of commerce) provide a matrix containing the value of commodity flows between each pair of approximately 500 private-sector, intermediate IO industries.

Following the method of Fan and Lang (2000) or Fan and Goyal (2006), we identify vertically forward or backward related industries by dividing a_{ij} by the dollar value of industry j's total output to get v_{ij}. This coefficient represents the dollar value of industry i's output necessary to produce one dollar's worth of industry j's output. We match this relatedness coefficient with the primary business segment of acquirer and target firms as reported by Worldscope. In contrast to Fan and Lang (2000), we do not base our analysis on a scale measure of relatedness, but use a cutoff point of coefficient v_{ij} larger than one percent to classify vertical relatedness (Sharur 2005; Fan and Goyal 2006; Kale and Shahrur 2007). Matching the industry of the input-output tables with the SIC code classification (industry level data), we are able to classify target and acquirer companies according to their vertical forward or backward relatedness. Similarly, we measure complementarity between acquirer's and target's industry by examining a potential overlap in their sourcing markets or sales markets. To calculate forward/backward complementarity coefficients, we determine the correlation corr(b_{ik}, b_{jk}) of the input/output of industries i and j supplied to each industry, where b_{ik} and b_{jk} are calculated as the percentage of each industry's output supplied to any other industry k. A large correlation coefficient suggests a substantial overlap in industries and markets to which industries i and j source or sell their products (Fan and Lang 2000). We do not base our analysis on a scale measure of complementarity, but identify forward and backward complementarity using a cut-off point of coefficient corr(b_{ik}, b_{jk}) larger than 50 percent.[24]

Summarizing, we distinguish three types of relatedness: (1) horizontal relatedness, (2) vertical relatedness (forward and backward), and (3) complementary relatedness (forward and backward). We classify two businesses as horizontally related if they operate in the same industry (same primary four-digit SIC). We define businesses as vertically related that are non-horizontally related, but that use the other's services or products as input/output for their own production (vertical

[24] The calculation of inter-industry relatedness is calculated based on data as defined by Fan and Lang (2000) and published by the Chinese University Hong Kong. For a detailed description of IO-table information and methodology to extract relatedness and complementary coefficients see Fan and Lang (2000).

forward/backward relatedness coefficient v_{ij} is larger than one percent). We identify two businesses as complementary if they are non-horizontally related and have a high overlap in the markets they source their input from or they sell their products to (forward/backward complementarity coefficient $corr(b_{ik}, b_{jk})$ is larger than 50 percent). The remaining transactions are classified as diversifying mergers. To test robustness of findings, we account for relatedness effects across primary and secondary segments, as many mergers are between primary and secondary business segments of firms (Maksimovic and Philipps 2001). Table 3.1 and 3.2 provide descriptive statistics on the data sample.

Table 3.1 Descriptive statistics on continuous and binary variables

This table describes the data collected for the description of relatedness, industry characteristics, deal characteristics, and acquirer characteristics. Proportions are reported for binary variables. Mean, median, standard deviation, minimum, and maximum are reported for continuous variables.

Variable name	N	Proportion	Mean	Median	Stdev.	Minimum	Maximum
Measures of relatedness (based on primary segment information)							
Horizontal merger	65	19.7%	-	-	-	-	-
Diversifying merger	175	53.0%	-	-	-	-	-
Vertical/complementary merger	90	27.3%	-	-	-	-	-
Measures of relatedness (based on primary and secondary segment information)							
Horizontal merger	106	32.1%	-	-	-	-	-
Diversifying merger	121	36.7%	-	-	-	-	-
Vertical/complementary merger	103	31.2%	-	-	-	-	-
Deal characteristics							
Transaction size	330	-	241.4	68.2	903.8	20.0	14,052
Relative size	317	-	32.4%	11.9%	72.2%	0.2%	861.1%
Industry characteristics							
Industry growth	330	-	4.3%	4.2%	3.4%	-17.4%	12.8%
Industry concentration	330	-	0.12	0.11	0.89	0.09	0.84
Acquirer characteristics							
Prior performance acquirer	309	-	5.6%	-1.1%	59.5%	-94.4%	614.4%
Prior experience	75	22.7%	-	-	-	-	-
Prior vertical experience	25	7.6%	-	-	-	-	-
Prior diversifying experience	112	33.9%	-	-	-	-	-

Table 3.2 Distribution of transactions by industry and transaction type

This table provides descriptive data on industry composition and relatedness classification of transactions. Relatedness classification is based on primary and secondary segment information.

Industry	Primary SIC Code Acquirer	Number of transactions	horizontal	vertical /compl.	divers. /lateral
A. Engines and turbines					
Turbines and turbine generator sets	3511	10	8	2	-
Internal combustion engines, nec.	3519	3	-	2	1
B. Farm and garden machinery and equipment					
Farm machinery and equipment	3523	20	9	4	7
Lawn and garden tractors and equipment	3524	2	1	1	-
C. Construction, mining, and materials handling					
Construction machinery and equipment	3531	18	8	8	2
Mining mach. & equip., except oil and gas	3532	4	3	-	1
Conveyors and conveying equipment	3535	15	7	-	8
Hoists, cranes, monorail systems	3536	8	2	5	1
Ind. trucks, tractors, trailers, & stackers	3537	7	1	5	1
D. Metalworking machinery and equipment					
Machine tools, metal cutting types	3541	19	5	6	8
Machine tools, metal forming types	3542	3	1	-	2
Special dies, tools, and jigs and fixtures	3544	2	-	1	1
Cutting tools and machine tool accessories	3545	8	4	-	4
Power-driven hand tools	3546	4	2	1	1
Electric & gas welding & soldering equip.	3548	3	2	1	-
Metalworking machinery, nec	3549	2	-	-	2
E. Special ind. machinery, exc. metalworking					
Textile machinery	3552	7	2	1	4
Woodworking machinery	3553	2	-	2	-
Paper industries machinery	3554	5	1	2	2
Printing trades machinery	3555	7	1	2	4
Food products machinery	3556	2	1	1	-
Special industry machinery, nec	3559	36	7	15	14
F. General industrial machinery and equipment					
Pumps and pumping equipment	3561	16	5	9	2
Air and gas compressors	3563	9	5	2	2
Ind. and commercial fans and blowers	3564	3	2	1	-
Packaging machinery	3565	15	3	6	6
Industrial process furnaces and ovens	3567	2	-	-	2
Mechanical power transmission equip., nec	3568	4	1	1	2
General industrial machinery and equip.	3569	29	6	5	18
G. Refrigeration and service industry machinery					
Automatic vending machines	3581	2	1	-	1
Refrigeration and heating equipment	3585	30	8	15	7
Measuring and dispensing pumps	3586	1	-	-	1
Service industry machines, nec	3589	8	3	4	1
H. Miscellaneous industrial and commercial					
Fluid power cylinders and actuators	3593	13	3	-	10
Fluid power pumps and motors	3594	6	2	1	3
Scales and balances, except laboratory	3596	1	1	-	-
Machinery, except electrical	3599	4	1	-	3
Total		330	106	103	121

3.3.4 Explanation of cross-sectional influence factors

To explain why different merger strategies develop, we need to generate an understanding of wealth creation mechanism in mergers of machinery manufacturers. We analyze wealth determinants by applying several cross-sectional factors that are closely related to industry-specific and theoretical motives as discussed in the literature review. We include three different sets of characteristics: deal, industry, and acquirer characteristics.

Deal characteristics include two control variables related to the transaction size. "Deal value" is likely to affect potential synergy and market power implications. For example, Cornett, McNutt, and Tehranian (2006) find in an analysis of the banking industry that large bank mergers are associated with greater performance than small bank mergers. Wilcox, Chang, and Grover (2001) observe the same for an analysis in the telecommunications industry. Helwege, Pirinsky, and Stulz (2007) relate this to a positive information effect. They assume that larger firms are more frequently monitored by analysts, investors, and regulators reducing the risk of overvaluation and integration of the company. On the other hand, Moeller, Schlingemann, and Stulz (2004) show that a high deal size can be associated with hubris or agency problems, as managers want to maximize their own utility. The second variable is "relative size of acquisition", measured as the ratio of deal size to bidder's market value at T_{-21} before the announcement day of the merger. Asquit, Bruner, and Mullins (1983) report that bidder returns increase with the ratio of target to bidder equity capitalization. Mulherin and Boone (2000) assume that the wealth effects for both acquisitions and divestitures are directly related to the relative size of the event.

To assess the impact of relatedness between target and acquirer company, we control for the industry background of transaction participants including the two variables "industry growth" and "industry concentration". We calculate industry growth based on sales data we obtain through the Thomson One Banker database (four-digit SIC level). According to Clelland, Douglas, and Henderson (2006), there will be a higher level of competition in an industry with a lower growth rate reflecting an increasingly zero-sum game of mutual dependence. A lower growth rate may also limit strategic options of the firm and thus increase pressure to act. "Industry concentration" plays an important part in determining market power, business behavior, and performance of companies (Curry and George 1983). In addition, it is a suitable measure of barriers to entry (Hou and Robinson 2006). Shan and Wilson (2007) argue that industry concentration has a direct influence on abnormal stock returns. Mpoyi (2003) assumes that industry characteristics significantly affect vertical integration strategies of companies. We measure market concentration as a sales-based Herfindahl-Hirschman index (HHI) on a four-digit SIC level to classify different sub-industries.

Apart from industry characteristic, we examine acquirer characteristics as determinants of merger success. These variables characterize the individual position of acquirers and may help to explain why machinery companies apply different strategies in merger situations. We examine the influence of two key variables, the first focusing on the performance of the acquirer, the second reflecting the experience of the acquirer in managing an integrated value chain or diversified business segments. As performance indicator we measure the historical stock price performance as a buy and hold return of acquirer stocks relative to a specific index return (relevant country-specific Datastream machinery index) over the estimation period (T_{-300} to T_{-50}). To measure experience of acquirers, we analyze available segment information on Worldscope database to examine whether at the time of announcement the acquirer was already diversified, vertically integrated, or complementary structured. Kahle and Walkling (1996) find that the Compustat industry classification does not account for the fact that many firms change their primary SIC code over time. To avoid this dilution, we use available historical segment information to identify the business segments of the acquirer at the time of the transaction announcement. Hayward (2002) shows that acquirer's focal acquisition performance positively relates to prior acquisitions. Also Finkelstein and Haleblian (2002) suggest that the routines and practices established in prior situations transfer to new situations and that the effect of such transfers depends on the similarity of industrial environments. To detect vertical and complementary integration experience, we follow the same method using commodity flow data and calculate inter-industry relations as described in section 3.2 (Fan and Lang 2000).

Table 3.3 Variable definition and source description

This table contains the definitions and data sources for each variable collected for the four categories measures of relatedness, deal characteristics, industry characteristics, and acquirer characteristics.

Variable name	Definition	Sources
Measures of relatedness		
Relatedness	Dummy variable that equals one if the transaction is either vertical related, horizontal, or complementary.	Thomson One Banker, Bureau of Econo. Analy.
Horizontal	Dummy variable that equals one if the acquirer and target company share the same primary four-digit SIC.	Thomson One Banker, Bureau of Econo. Analy.
Vertical	Dummy variable that equals one if the transaction is non-horizontal and either forward or vertically related.	Thomson One Banker, Bureau of Econo. Analy.
Vertical forward	Dummy variable if the transaction is non-horizontal and vertical forward relatedness coefficient v_{ij} is larger than one percent.	Thomson One Banker, Bureau of Econo. Analy.
Vertical backward	Dummy variable if the transaction is non-horizontal and vertical backward relatedness coefficient v_{ij} is larger than one percent.	Thomson One Banker, Bureau of Econo. Analy.
Complemen-tarity	Dummy variable that equals one if the transaction is non-horizontal and forward or vertically complem.	Thomson One Banker, Bureau of Econo. Analy.
Forward com-plementarity	Dummy variable that equals one if the transaction is non-horizontal and the forward complementarity coefficient corr(b_{ik}, b_{jk}) is larger than 50 percent.	Thomson One Banker, Bureau of Econo. Analy.
Backward complemen-tarity	Dummy variable that equals one if the transaction is non-horizontal and the backward complementarity coefficient corr(b_{ik}, b_{jk}) is larger than 50 percent.	Thomson One Banker, Bureau of Econo. Analy.
Deal characteristics		
Deal value	Transaction volume of the transaction.	Datastream
Relative deal size	The transaction size divided by the acquirer's market value at T_{-21}.	Datastream

Table 3.3 (continued)

Variable Name	Definition	Sources
Industry characteristics		
Industry growth	Average last-three-year growth rate of the acquirer primary four-digit SIC (aggregated sales information).	Thomson One Banker (Public Company)
Industry concentration	Measure of the prevailing industry concentration using the sales based Herfindahl-Hirschman index (HHI).	Thomson One Banker (Public and Private Company)
Acquirer characteristics		
Prior perform. acquirer	The buy and hold return of the acquirer relative to the specific stock index over the estimation period.	Datastream
Experience	Dummy variable that equals one if the acquirer was either diversified or vertically integrated at the time of the transaction announcement.	Worldscope
Vertical experience	Dummy variable that equals one if the acquirer was vertically integrated at the time of the transaction announcement (relatedness coefficient v_{ij} larger one percent).	Worldscope, Bureau of Economic Analysis
Diversification experience	Dummy variable that equals one if the acquirer was diversified at the time of the transaction announcement.	Worldscope

3.4 Empirical results

3.4.1 Univariate analysis

Panel A of table 3.4 provides an overview of abnormal announcement period returns for the full sample of machinery mergers. Results show that significant wealth gains accrue to both shareholders of target and bidding firms. We observe statistically significant results for all of our six event windows with target gains of 17.4 percent to 21.2 percent while acquirer's shareholders profit between 1.7 percent and 2.3 percent. Wealth effects for combined entity show positive results while rival returns react statistically significant in the [-10;+10] event window only (positive effect of 0.91 percent). The absence of wealth transfers between target and acquirer shareholders strengthens the assumption that mergers in the machinery industry are not motivated by management hubris or agency problems (Berkovitch and Narayanan 1993). The findings may indicate that significant synergy gains or collusive rents are available to merging companies.

Table 3.4 Excess stock returns to machinery manufacturers

This table shows the average cumulative abnormal return for the total sample of 330 mergers in the machinery industry during 1997-2007 for six different event windows. The statistical significance is tested using the test-statistics of Boehmer, Musumeci, and Poulsen (1991) (z-statistic). Statistical significance at the 1%, 5%, and 10% level is denoted with ***, **, and * respectively.

Event window	Target (N = 58)		Acquirer (N = 309)		CWE (N = 56)		Rivals (N = 287)	
	CAAR	z-stat.	CAAR	z-stat.	CAAR	z-stat.	CAAR	z-stat.
[-1/+1]	17.43%	7.17***	1.67%	4.65***	2.84%	2.67**	-0.12%	-0.63
[-3+1]	19.15%	7.42***	1.91%	5.06***	2.78%	2.38**	0.08%	0.47
[-3/+3]	19.08%	6.95***	1.96%	5.54***	2.51%	2.47**	0.02%	0.48
[-5+1]	20.74%	6.60***	2.21%	5.16***	3.71%	2.73***	0.18%	0.58
[-5/+5]	20.50%	6.13***	2.28%	4.23***	3.50%	2.35**	0.10%	0.50
[-10/+10]	21.21%	6.83***	1.76%	2.94***	3.35%	2.15**	0.91%	1.96*

To examine univariate effects of relatedness between target and acquirer and to test our hypotheses on wealth creation, we perform a subsample analysis presented in tables 3.5. Consistent with our initial hypothesis, abnormal returns to acquiring firms and combined entity are higher for horizontal transactions compared to unrelated transactions. Target abnormal returns for horizontal transactions are lower and statistically different from diversifying transactions implying that the strategic premium for a consolidation in the machinery industry is low. This partially contradicts findings of Churyk and Baker (2004) who elaborate that the amount of premiums paid by the acquiring companies to the acquired companies are not related to the degree of industrial associations between the companies.

Table 3.5 Subsample analysis relatedness – primary segments

This table shows the average cumulative abnormal return for the subsample analysis of 330 mergers in the machinery industry during 1997-2007. The statistical significance is tested using the test-statistics of Boehmer, Musumeci, and Poulsen (1991) (z-statistic). Statistical significance at the 1%, 5%, and 10% level is denoted with ***, **, and * respectively.

	Unrelated			Vertical/Complementary			Horizontal		
	N	CAAR	z-stat.	N	CAAR	z-stat.	N	CAAR	z-stat.
Event window [-1;+1]									
Target	30	20.05	5.91***	17	18.59%	3.46***	11	8.51%[b]	2.81**
Acquirer	160	1.33%	2.99***	89	1.97%	2.59**	60	2.14%	2.52**
CWE	28	1.57%	0.82	17	4.30%	3.18***	11	3.82%	2.12*
Rival	147	-0.02%	-0.24	75	-0.06%	-0.08	65	-0.41%	-0.94
Event window [-5;+5]									
Target	30	26.42	5.47***	17	18.88%	2.83**	11	6.88%[b]	1.91*
Acquirer	160	1.35%	2.47**	89	3.55%	2.48**	60	2.88%	2.63**
CWE	28	3.11%	1.54	17	4.52%	1.58	11	2.94%	0.77
Rival	147	0.06%	0.16	75	0.23%	0.56	65	0.03%	0.22
Event window [-10;+10]									
Target	30	24.92	5.59***	17	19.25%	3.26***	11	14.10	2.9**
Acquirer	160	1.17%	1.85*	89	1.60%	1.050	60	3.59%	2.47**
CWE	28	2.73%	1.38	17	2.29%	1.91*	11	6.55%	0.82
Rival	147	0.68%	0.89	75	1.31%	1.48	65	0.97%	1.15

[a] The average abnormal return between related and unrelated transactions is significantly different at the 10% level
[b] The average abnormal return between related and unrelated transactions is significantly different at the 5% level
[c] The average abnormal return between related and unrelated transactions is significantly different at the 1% level

Furthermore, when taking into account secondary segments (table 3.6) results show that acquirer abnormal returns are statistically significantly higher in horizontal transactions compared with diversifying transactions. We interpret this as a signal of positive relatedness implications in mergers. For rival reactions, we do not detect significant differences according to the form of relatedness.

Table 3.6 Subsample analysis relatedness – primary/secondary segments

This table shows the average cumulative abnormal return for the subsample analysis of 330 mergers in the machinery industry during 1997-2007. The statistical significance is tested using the test-statistics of Boehmer, Musumeci, and Poulsen (1991) (z-statistic). Statistical significance at the 1%, 5%, and 10% level is denoted with ***, **, and * respectively.

	Unrelated			Vertical/Complementary			Horizontal		
	N	CAAR	z-stat.	N	CAAR	z-stat.	N	CAAR	z-stat.
Event window [-1;+1]									
Target	18	23.93	5.62***	19	18.65	3.81***	21	10.76%	3.33***
Acquirer	110	1.17%	2.46**	10	1.41%	2.24**	99	2.50%	3.51***
CWE	18	1.87%	0.90	19	2.46%	1.05	19	4.15%	2.66**
Rival	106	0.05%	0.18	86	0.11%	0.28	95	-0.52%	-1.68*
Event window [-5;+5]									
Target	18	31.27	4.72***	19	19.46	3.10***	21	16.96%	4.26***
Acquirer	110	0.73%	1.71*	10	3.05%	2.43**	99	2.36%[b]	2.94***
CWE	18	3.86%	1.70	19	2.17%	0.85	19	3.95%	1.41
Rival	106	0.35%	0.87	86	0.25%	-0.50	95	0.32%	0.86
Event window [-10;+10]									
Target	18	29.41	4.74***	19	19.59	3.62***	21	15.64%	4.35***
Acquirer	110	0.38%	1.02	10	2.09%	1.64	99	2.96%[a]	2.67***
CWE	18	2.99%	1.20	19	2.66%	2.05*	19	4.37%	0.88
Rival	106	0.95%	1.38	86	1.03%	1.02	95	0.75%	0.98

[a] The average abnormal return between related and unrelated transactions is significantly different at the 10% level
[b] The average abnormal return between related and unrelated transactions is significantly different at the 5% level
[c] The average abnormal return between related and unrelated transactions is significantly different at the 1% level

Vertical transactions show a more differentiated picture. Although acquirer wealth gains in vertical/complementary transactions are higher than in unrelated transactions for all three event windows (tables 3.5 and 3.6), the difference is statistically not significant. Overall wealth creation of the combined entity also shows an ambiguous pattern. Therefore, we divide vertical/complementary transactions into two subsamples of backward and forward oriented relatedness considering secondary segment information (table 3.7).[25] Consistent with our description of market trends, capital markets prefer forward vertical/complementary transactions. This is true for target, acquirer, and combined entity abnormal returns, however, the difference in wealth creation is only statistically significant for combined entity returns. Although the small sample size requires to interpret the findings with some caution, the result suggests that machinery manufacturers who do not limit their product portfolio to the production process, but use M&A transactions to integrate upstream services are more successful in capital market performance.

In this context, vertical forward or complementary forward relatedness may generate a similar positive capital market evaluation as horizontal transactions. The opposite is true for backward oriented vertical or complementary transactions, as results show that those are least appreciated by capital markets. A possible explanation may be that business activities in downstream industries may not provide sufficient advantages to machinery companies probably because increased complexity of integration overweight benefits such as reduced transaction costs or residual rights of control. This seems also reflected in the overall low target premium (target abnormal returns equal 12.8 percent) that machinery manufacturers are willing to pay for vertical/complementary backward related firms.

---

[25] An analysis based on primary segment information does not provide sufficient data.

Table 3.7 Subsample analysis on forward and backward integration

This table shows a subsample analysis of cumulative abnormal return for the total sample of 330 mergers in the machinery industry during 1997-2007, relatedness classification based on primary and secondary business segment. The statistical significance is tested using the test-statistics of Boehmer, Musumeci, and Poulsen (1991) (z-statistic). Statistical significance at the 1%, 5%, and 10% level is denoted with ***, **, and *.

Event window [-1;+1]	Target		Acquirer		CWE		Rivals	
	N	CAAR	N	CAAR	N	CAAR	N	CAAR
Unrelated mergers	18	23.93%	110	1.17%	18	1.87%	106	0.05%
z-stat.		*5.62****		*2.46***		*0.90*		*0.18*
Backward vert./comp.[1)]	14	12.80%[a]	84	1.25%	14	0.25%	73	0.12%
z-stat.		*2.67***		*1.70**		*0.22*		*0.12*
Forward vert./comp.[1)]	5	35.04%	16	2.27%	5	8.64%[a]	13	0.09%
z-stat.		*3.21**		*2.35***		*3.41***		*0.58*
Horizontal mergers	21	10.76%[b]	99	2.50%	19	4.15%	95	-0.52%
z-stat.		*3.33****		*3.51****		*2.66***		*-1.68**

[a] The average abnormal return between related and unrelated transactions is significantly different at the 10% level
[b] The average abnormal return between related and unrelated transactions is significantly different at the 5% level
[1)] Results for backward and forward vertical/complementary transactions differ for combined entity returns at the 10% level

In sum, our initial hypothesis that relatedness between target and acquirer influences wealth creation finds empirical support. Abnormal returns are by far highest for horizontal transactions, although target's strategic premium is surprisingly low. For vertical/complementary transactions, reactions are twofold as the direction of the takeover is important. Backward orientation does not create value while forward integration shows the highest wealth creation for both, acquirer and combined entity shareholders. Our results confirm recent empirical evidence of the influence of relatedness between target and acquirer (e.g. Seth 1990; Comment and Jarrell 1995; Walker 2000) and contradict other studies that reject this influence (e.g. Lubatkin 1987; Kaplan and Weisenbach 1992). To support the observations of univariate analysis and to filter dilution effects, we examine industry and control variables jointly and conduct a multivariate analysis.

3.4.2 *Cross-sectional regression analysis*

We perform multivariate analyses of defined variables to jointly measure effects of relatedness on shareholder value using cumulative abnormal announcement returns over the [-1;+1] and the [-10;+10] event window as dependent variable.[26] The cross-sectional analysis examines cumulative abnormal returns of acquirers as we want to gain insights into corresponding wealth dynamics in mergers. We distinguish two different types of relatedness classification to strengthen robustness of the results (primary segment and primary/secondary segments). For each classification we build three different models to test for the impact of relatedness. Model I shows the greatest degree of abstraction as it refrains from distinguishing different types of relatedness. This abstraction level is refined in model II where horizontal, vertical, and complementary relatedness is considered. Model III additionally examines the influence of the direction (forward or backward) of complementary and vertical relatedness. We compute all test statistics using White's (1980) heteroskedasticity-consistent covariance matrix. The results are shown in table 3.8 and 3.9.

In the analysis of primary segment classification (table 3.8), the regression analysis provides further evidence of the influence of relatedness on wealth creation in mergers. Observing acquirer CARs in model I, the variable relatedness shows a significantly positive influence on acquirer wealth creation. When refining the relatedness definition in models II and III, the positive influence of relatedness is further detailed. Horizontal transactions show strongly positive influence on abnormal announcement returns (model II), highlighting a positive effect of transaction synergies and/or market power. The results also show a negative influence of vertically oriented transactions. However, the negative wealth effect is mainly attributed to negative influence of vertical backward oriented mergers (model III). Supporting the results of the univariate analysis, vertical backward integration is significantly negatively related to abnormal returns while vertical upstream integration shows positive influence on

[26] These two event windows represent the smallest and largest event window considered in this study, cross-sectional regressions for the remaining event windows show similar results.

value creation for acquirers (significant at five percent level for acquirer CAR in the [-1;+1] event window). These findings are also robust when taking into account secondary segments (table 3.9). The coefficients on complementary transactions do not yield clear results. While a general positive influence of complementarity is observed when considering secondary segments, the coefficient in the primary segment analysis turns negative.

All models confirm that deal characteristics are important determinants of wealth creation, as the proxy variables deal value and relative deal size are highly significant across all our models (I-III). Contradicting empirical findings stipulating a positive correlation between target size and acquirer returns (Wilcox, Chang, and Grover 2001; Fuller, Netter, and Stegemoller 2002; Cornett, McNutt, and Tehranian 2006), we observe a negative size effect reflecting potential implications such as increased financial and integration risk, but also potential hubris or agency problems. Surprisingly, the relative size of the transaction has an overall positive impact consistent with findings of other empirical studies (Asquith, Bruner, and Mullins 1983; Mulherin and Boone 2000). Similar to Moeller, Schlingemann, and Stulz (2004), we argue that absolute smaller acquirers with relative larger targets are more prone to realize positive acquirer gains.

In contrast to our expectations, industry variables do not appear to have a significant influence on excess returns. However, the negative coefficient of industry growth is in line with our assumption, as in slow growing industries the decision to merge should be higher valued by capital markets than in fast growing industries, as pressure to act as well as competition levels are higher (Clelland, Douglas, and Henderson 2006). The negative correlation of industry concentration with acquirer returns indicates that mergers in highly concentrated industries are less appreciated by capital markets and that gains from potential industry collusion may be comparably low.

Finally, acquirer characteristics show significant impact on return behavior. Prior performance of acquirers (measured as the buy and hold return during the estimation period) is significantly negatively related to acquirer abnormal returns indicating a potential dilution effect of acquirer performance in merger situations. For well performing acquirers, capital markets potentially assume integration risks associated with the transaction leading to less overall wealth creation in mergers. The firm's experience and capacity to manage additional complexity induced by the merger shows a positive connection to acquirer excess returns. Firms that are already diversified at the time of the transaction announcement generate more overall wealth than "inexperienced" firms (model II-III), potentially because of firms' internal know-how to successfully manage the integration. Findings are robust when taking into account secondary segments (table 3.9).

Table 3.8 Multivariate analysis of acquirer CAR – primary segments

Relatedness classification based on primary business segments. We test different models, where model I has the greatest degree of abstraction as it does not distinguish between different types of relatedness. The abstraction level is refined in model II distinguishing horizontal, vertical, and complementary transactions. Model III examines the influence of forward or backward orientation. The test statistic is computed using White's (1980) heteroskedasticity-consistent covariance matrix. Statistical significance at the 1%, 5%, and 10% level is denoted with ***, **, and * respectively.

	Dep. Variable: CAAR [-1;+1]			Dep. Variable: CAAR [-10;+10]		
Variable name	Model I	Model II	Model III	Model I	Model II	Model III
Intercept	0.036	0.043	0.044	0.037	0.052	0.050
	*2.485***	*2.552****	*2.790****	*1.416*	*1.607*	*1.745**
Measures of Relatedness						
Relatedness	0.013			0.024		
	*1.784**			*1.827**		
Horizontal		0.020			0.049	
		*1.955**			*2.667****	
Vertical		-0.019			-0.025	
		-1.057			*-0.899*	
Forward vertical			0.063			0.080
			*2.132***			*1.880**
Backward vertical			-0.053			-0.058
			*-1.822**			*-1.418*
Complementarity		0.019			0.002	
		0.932			*0.062*	
Forward complementary			-0.011			0.000
			-0.571			*0.009*
Backward complementary			-0.058			-0.072
			*-1.910**			*-1.635*
Deal characteristics						
Deal value	-0.000	-0.000	-0.000	-0.000	-0.000	-0.000
	*-2.003***	*-2.249***	*-2.332***	*-2.166***	*-2.363****	*-2.392***
Log relative size	0.026	0.028	0.027	0.040	0.041	0.042
	*2.996****	*3.020****	*3.036****	*2.446***	*2.511****	*2.383***
Industry characteristics						
Industry growth	0.038	0.032	0.031	0.019	0.005	0.010
	1.043	*0.818*	*0.777*	*0.567*	*0.129*	*0.285*
Industry concentr.	-0.028	-0.044	-0.033	0.012	-0.015	0.007
	-0.708	*-1.090*	*-0.849*	*0.176*	*-0.207*	*0.099*

Table 3.8 (continued)

	Dep. Variable: CAAR [-1;+1]			Dep. Variable: CAAR [-10;+10]		
	Model I	Model II	Model III	Model I	Model II	Model III
Acquirer characteristics						
Prior performance	-0.022 *-3.845******	-0.024 *-3.723******	-0.023 *-3.580******	-0.053 *-3.387******	-0.057 *-3.409******	-0.055 *-3.266******
Experience	0.012 *1.205*			0.033 *1.750**		
Vertical experience		-0.007 *-0.580*	-0.009 *-0.755*		-0.017 *-0.891*	-0.021 *-1.042*
Diversifying experience		0.022 *1.579*	0.020 *1.472*		0.051 *1.908**	0.043 *1.693**
N	250	250	250	250	250	250
Adj. R squared	0.094	0.095	0.087	0.095	0.106	0.083

Table 3.9 Multivariate analysis of acquirer CAR – primary/secondary segments

Relatedness classification based on primary and secondary business segments. We test different models, where model I has the greatest degree of abstraction as it does not distinguish between different types of relatedness. The abstraction level is refined in model II distinguishing horizontal, vertical, and complementary transactions. Model III examines the influence of forward or backward orientation. The test statistic is computed using White's (1980) heteroskedasticity-consistent covariance matrix. Statistical significance at the 1%, 5%, and 10% level is denoted with ***, **, and * respectively.

	Dep. Variable: CAAR [-1;+1]			Dep. Variable: CAAR [-10;+10]		
Variable name	Model I	Model II	Model III	Model I	Model II	Model III
Intercept	0.039	0.043	0.044	0.034	0.038	0.047
	*2.633****	*2.685****	*2.735****	*1.247*	*2.355****	*1.578*
Measures of Relatedness						
Relatedness	0.007			0.027		
	0.965			*1.901**		
Horizontal		0.011			0.026	
		1.340			*1.868**	
Vertical		-0.014			-0.039	
		-1.304			*-1.982***	
Forward vertical			-0.021			-0.019
			-1.457			*-0.831*
Backward vertical			-0.010			-0.035
			-0.902			*-1.768**
Complementarity		0.004			0.028	
		0.452			*1.656**	
Forward complementary			0.016			0.028
			1.171			*1.526*
Backward complementary			0.007			0.030
			0.731			*1.661**
Deal characteristics						
Deal value	-0.000	-0.000	-0.000	-0.000	-0.000	-0.000
	*-2.198***	*-2.649****	*-2.326****	*-2.361***	*-2.722****	*-2.355***
Log relative size	0.026	0.029	0.028	0.041	0.045	0.045
	*3.025****	*3.125****	*3.059****	*2.475***	*2.567****	*2.499***
Industry characteristics						
Industry growth	0.037	0.031	0.033	0.020	0.007	0.012
	1.010	*0.845*	*0.903*	*0.590*	*0.187*	*0.345*
Industry concentr.	-0.032	-0.040	-0.035	0.007	-0.003	0.009
	-0.822	*-1.010*	*-0.865*	*0.103*	*-0.042*	*0.131*

Table 3.9 (continued)

	Dep. Variable: CAAR [-1;+1]			Dep. Variable: CAAR [-1;+1]		
	Model I	Model II	Model III	Model I	Model II	Model III
Acquirer characteristics						
Prior performance	-0.022 *-3.810****	-0.023 *-3.739****	-0.024 *-3.857****	-0.053 *-3.382****	-0.055 *-3.384****	-0.056 *-3.413****
Experience	0.012 *1.228*			0.033 *1.777**		
Vertical experience		-0.006 *-0.525*	-0.009 *-0.709*		-0.019 *-0.933*	-0.023 *-1.125*
Diversifying experience		0.023 *1.645*	0.022 *1.560*		0.050 *1.917**	0.048 *1.799**
N	250	307	250	250	250	250
Adj. R squared	0.088	0.094	0.091	0.096	0.110	0.101

3.5 Summary and conclusion

Our objective in this paper is to add to the ongoing discussion of corporate focus and diversification examining the role of corporate relatedness in wealth creation for machinery mergers. Answering recent criticisms that highlight sample selection effects (Campa and Kedia 2002; Gomes and Livdan 2004), the disregard of different industry logics and drivers (Fowler and Schmidt 1988; Mitchell and Mulherin 1996), and methodological shortcoming of relatedness classification (Fan and Goyal 2006), we examine the role of relatedness in mergers of machinery manufacturers. As this industry compromises strongly varying business strategies with regard to concentration on core business, diversification, and vertical integration, we test how capital markets evaluate different types of relatedness in merger situations and try to identify dominant strategies. To avoid weaknesses of classical methodologies of relatedness classification, we apply the approach of Fan and Lang (2000) using commodity flow data to determine forward/backward vertical and complementary relationships.

We find empirical support for the positive influence of corporate focus in mergers. Differentiating between horizontal, vertical/complementary, and unrelated transactions, relatedness has significant positive influence on wealth creation and excess returns. However, the discussion on the right corporate focus should account for vertical integration strategies of firms. While there is little empirical work on vertical mergers, the lack of knowledge of those implications makes a full assessment of the diversifying mergers difficult (Fan and Goyal 2006). As we observe, forward integration shows significant wealth creation potential for acquirer and combined entity shareholders (similar to horizontal transactions) while backward orientation is hardly value generating. Considering short-term capital market evaluations, our results confirm that managers can make choices to materially influence the profitability of mergers (Brunner 2002). Machinery manufacturers should therefore not limit their corporate focus to the production process only, but integrate upstream services in their product portfolio. This facilitates their transformation towards system providers allowing for an influence on the demand side and a potential reduction of production complexity. Nonetheless, our results also suggest that diversification is value increasing for acquirer firms rejecting the long-standing proposition that diversification destroys value.

The cross-sectional regression further strengthens the findings of the univariate analysis. Controlling for factors such as deal characteristics, industry characteristics, and acquirer characteristics, we observe that relatedness plays a major role in determining wealth in machinery mergers. The results are also robust when taking into account secondary business segments of acquirer and target firms. Our analysis shows that acquirer's performance and experience have a significant influence on the success of a transaction. Companies that are already diversified or vertically related at the time of merger announcement are able to generate more wealth in M&A transactions.

Our findings contribute to the existing literature in two ways: First, we provide an industry-specific perspective on corporate focus and diversification. We find that researchers and practitioners implicitly need to consider the right vertical integration strategy towards downstream or upstream industries in corporate focus discussions. Second, besides relatedness, we find that the individual characteristics of target and acquirer firms are significant wealth determinants in transactions underlining managements' role of target selection and target integration.

4 Horizontal acquisitions, merger rents, and non-price competition – a case study from the machinery industry

4.1 Introduction

Direct claims that a merger is executed to achieve market power are rare, as market rents are often seen as attempts by merging firms to expropriate wealth from customers by limiting output, raising product prices, and/or lowering factor prices (Stigler 1964; Chatterjee 1986; Trautwein 1990; Sharur 2005). Even though impact on social welfare can be offset by an increase in non-price variables (Eckbo 1983; Focarelli and Panetta 2003), it is difficult for economic researchers with their coarse information set to really understand the implicit nature of market power synergies (Andrade, Mitchell, and Stafford 2001; Pautler 2001). We circumvent the methodological shortcomings of larger empirical studies and examine the sources and mechanics of market power effects by focusing on the merger of Schuler and Mueller Weingarten, as this acquisition allows to illustrate strong evidence for market power rents and post-merger collusion.

On March 27, 2007, the press manufacturer Schuler announced the takeover of its major rival Mueller Weingarten (MW) creating a world market leader with approximately 35 percent market share in large mechanical and hydraulic presses (Metalworking Insiders' Report 2007). From the perspective of Schuler's management board, entering this transaction carried an opportunity to sustain the positioning of the company in the metal forming environment by strengthening its technological leadership and know-how, balancing its product portfolio, and extending its global coverage on future markets. After years of flat or declining sales growth and significant negative earnings,[27] the annual synergies of the transaction were estimated

[27] In its last fiscal year before the merger (05/06), Schuler reported losses of nearly EUR -9.5m on sales of around EUR 563m. MW realized losses of EUR -13.8m on sales of around EUR 336m in its fiscal year 2006.

at approximately EUR 35m. The merger was approved by antitrust authorities without constraints.

Through the merger Schuler became the clear technological leader in its core markets allowing it to stabilize price levels in the industry for metal forming products: *"Through the merger with MW the product prices increased, before the merger they were ruinous partly even below production costs"* (Tonn, CEO Schuler in Reuters 2009). After years of strong competition with MW, the merger allowed Schuler to move competition towards non-price variables such as technological differentiation, balanced product portfolio, and global service offerings allowing to realize significant market power effects in form of pricing synergies. This characteristic allows to select this case as particularly suitable for illuminating and extending relationships and logic among market power rents and their value creation effect in mergers (Eisenhardt and Graebner 2007).

Analyzing capital market reactions and accounting performance, we interpret the positive overall transaction evaluation of Schuler and MW as a reflection of attributed market power synergies. Being the market and innovation leader in the metal forming environment, Schuler is able to over-proportionally profit from the merger. Following the transaction, the market for metal forming products shows an increase in product prices allowing to improve Schuler's profit margins while at the same time increasing its order income. This becomes evident, when comparing the performance against Schuler's publicly listed peer competitors. Interpreting the highly negative rival abnormal returns upon the merger announcement, we observe that positive merger effects are, if at all, only to a lesser part available to rival companies. The successive improvement of relative performance figures as well as the positive order income development against competition confirm the picture of successful extortion of merger synergies for Schuler. Rival companies seem not to be able to imitate or to adapt quickly to changing competition parameters (non-price variables such as technological know-how and global service coverage). We conclude, if a competitive edge in non-price variables can be achieved that allows to circumvent pricing competition, mergers may lead to significant wealth creation for shareholders in connection with market power gains. Furthermore, if this competitive advantage cannot be imitated, market power rents are, in contrast to common interpretations of academic theory and empirical research, not necessarily available to competitors.

The remainder of the paper is structured as follows. We first introduce current literature focusing on theoretical and empirical findings regarding market power motives and effects (section 4.2). Based on a detailed description of the industry environment and transaction partners, we discuss underlying merger motivation and implied transaction synergies of the MW takeover by Schuler (section 4.3). In section 4.4, the performance of the acquirer is evaluated based on capital market and accounting data as opposed to a peer benchmark. The paper concludes with a summary and discussion of our findings (section 4.5).

4.2 Literature review and market characteristics

4.2.1 Literature review

The notion of price and concentration relationship is well entrenched in financial research, as market power synergies often imply severe price changes for customers and/or suppliers with inherent macroeconomic consequences. In so called price-concentration studies the pricing behavior of firms in relation to market consolidation and concentration is examined (Pautler 2001; Baker 2003). For example, Schmalensee (1987) observes through cross-section comparison involving markets in the same industry that seller concentration seems positively related to the level of price. Weiss (1989) examines price-concentration studies in several industries and, with one exception, finds price increases associated with increases in concentration. Also Neumark and Share (1992) provide empirical evidence showing that downward price rigidity and upward price flexibility are a consequence of market concentration in the banking industry since deposit interest rates are inversely related to the price charged by banks for deposits. Similar, Borenstein and Shepard (2002) examine wholesale price responses in 188 gasoline markets and find that firms with market power adjust prices slower than firms in high competition. In contrast, Wen (2001) finds no indication that the consolidation of the Canadian supermarket sector leads to relative food price increases or rising supermarket profitability.

However, research that focuses on the dynamic examination of market power motives in merger situations is more difficult, as those synergies are difficult to capture (Ficery, Herd, and Pursche 2007) and are seldom communicated publicly (Trautwein 1990). To detect underlying market power motives, research often focuses on indirect evidence of market power consequences of mergers observing the reactions of rival companies in the market. Under the market power or monopoly theory, competitors' stocks should rise upon an announcement (as rivals should also benefit from e.g. increased product prices and limited output) and drop if the merger is challenged or cancelled (Eckbo 1983; Chatterjee 1986; Fee and Thomas 2004; Sharur 2005). Jensen and Ruback (1983) summarize a number of event studies that deal with the effects of merger announcements and rejects the monopoly theory. In a recent study, Fee and Thomas (2004) find little evidence for market power in upstream and downstream product-market effects, analyzing a data set that identifies corporate customers, suppliers, and rivals of the firms initiating horizontal mergers. While research agrees that a general relationship between net present value of synergies and announcement returns exists (Comment and Jarrell 1995; Walker 2000; Houston, James, and Ryngaert 2001), research examining the relationship between market power rents and company's performance does not show clear results (for summaries see Ravenscraft and Scherer 1987; Trautwein 1990). Also event studies show a generally unfavorable relationship between market power motives and stock returns (for summaries see Trautwein 1990; Kaplan, Mitchell, and Wruck 1997; Fan and Goyal 2006). Trautwein (1990) concludes that the monopoly theory's record appears to be weak, as most studies show that the primary reason for mergers is not to achieve monopoly power.

Market power rents are synergies often associated with expropriating wealth from customers by limiting output, raising product prices, and/or lowering factor prices (Stigler 1964; Chatterjee 1986; Trautwein 1990; Sharur 2005). Examining price increases of mergers, research often concludes that a potential social welfare loss is connected to collusive mergers (Chatterjee 1986). However, a limitation to the factor price can be too short-sighted, as a social welfare loss from post-merger collusion on price can be entirely offset by an increase in competition of non-price variables such as product quality and service (Eckbo 1983). Furthermore, Focarelli and Panetta (2003) show that the general conclusion of empirical literature that in-market consolidation generates adverse price changes harming consumers, may fall too short by only observing short-term pricing impact. Using information on deposit rates of individual banks, they find strong evidence that, although consolidation does generate adverse price changes, these are temporary. In the long run, efficiency gains dominate over the market power effect leading in the end to more favorable prices for consumers.

4.2.2 *Market characteristics of the metal forming industry*

The metal forming industry is a highly specialized and globalized industry with a clear focus on metal sheet forming for the automotive industry (estimated worldwide market share of 85 percent).[28] Following Schuler experts and market information, annual market revenues are estimated at approximately EUR 3.4bn in 2004. Market development and growth statistics of the press market are characterized by a cyclicality that is driven by investment strategies of the automotive industry. Against the background of restructuring of Original Equipment Manufacturers (OEMs), decreasing investment volumes, and global market saturation, the cyclicality and market developments are reflected in firm revenues. In recent years, demand for metal forming products was dominated by Asian OEMs like Toyota and Hyundai while large Western OEMs (e.g. GM, Ford, Daimler, or Volkswagen) have postponed their investments in presses. The ongoing crisis in the automotive sector additionally impacts the investment pattern and demand for press technology. For press manufacturers this resulted in increasing low-tech competition in basically all market segments.

The metal sheet forming market can be clustered into four different segments: press plant manufacturing (large press segment), specialized products manufacturing, automation, and service. With approximately 35 percent market share, press plant manufacturing is the largest segment and is driven by the demand of OEMs and Tier 0.5/1 clients.[29] Consequently, market potential is closely connected to growth expectations of the automotive industry and its investment strategies. Furthermore, market growth for press manufacturers is also influenced by "technological" advances as demand for high-tech products such as high-tensile sheets, smaller production batches, and other technological trends is increasing. Similar to other automotive supplier industries, competition is strong among the limited number of suppliers with different competing business models: Technology leaders that try to develop their

[28] Metal sheet forming with press capacity of larger than 80 tons.
[29] Tier 0.5/1 clients are automotive suppliers directly supplying to OEMs.

lower segments and cost leaders that try to develop their technological competences. While the Asian region is primarily dominated by local press manufacturers,[30] Schuler and MW have leading positions in Europe and the US.

Specialized products manufacturing is estimated at around 26 percent market share with primarily "Tier n" or non-automotive clients.[31] The market is far more fragmented and less cyclical than press plant manufacturing and is dominated by regional demand and supply. Competition in niche markets is high as clients often demand low-tech and low-price products. One of the key trends is therefore the standardization of products and distribution over established sales networks. Applications in specialized products manufacturing are various and include, next to small presses, hydro-forming, toggle lever presses, and other applications such as coin or medal minting.

Automation is estimated at approximately 20 percent market share and consists of basically two different businesses: the simultaneous investment in press and automation (system invest) and the complementary/substituting investment in automation of existing presses (retrofit). While the market for system investments is closely related to developments on markets for plant manufacturing and specialized products, the retrofit market is expected to grow disproportionate because of cost-, technology-, and geographic trends. Competition is high as many specialized automation companies enter the market. For original press manufacturers, automation services are usually offered only for their press product portfolio while a distribution of automation for competitive products is difficult.

Service is an attractive market with high margins and growth potential, where press manufacturers serve approximately 25 percent of the market. Due to its high profitability, the dynamics of the market are high, as not only press manufacturers aggressively try to expand their market shares. Other competitors from the maintenance and repair industry increasingly offer services that include press

[30] For example, Aida, Komatsu or Kawasaki.
[31] Tier n clients are suppliers to automotive suppliers.

technology. A further trend, induced through cost saving programs of OEMS, is the partial or full outsourcing of plant maintenance to subcontractors, dislocation of automotive production to low cost countries, and shifting of value added to automotive suppliers.

To cope with these developments of increasing competition, challenging profit situations, and changing market requirements, M&A has been discovered as a successful strategy. For example, in December 2004 one of the top five press producers Aida Engineering, took over Italy based Manzoni Group (including the press brands of Manzoni and Rovetta) in order to strengthen Aida's presence in Europe (Metalworking Insiders' Report 2004). On a broader basis, Geiger, Schiereck, and Wald (2009) show for machinery industry mergers that M&A transactions are particularly suitable to fence against increasing cost pressure from low-cost competitors and globally sourcing customers while operational excellence and product innovation in production and development processes of machinery manufacturers is becoming more and more important. They observe positive target and acquirer shareholders returns, as an expression of synergy and earning potential.

4.3 Case study background

4.3.1 Characterization of transaction partners

Schuler

Schuler has its origins in 1839 when it was founded by Louis Schuler in Göppingen, Germany, to construct machine tools for sheet metal processing. Initial growth was largely driven by innovations in mechanical press technology, for example by introducing the world's first eccentric and drawing presses with mechanical drives in 1879 or by delivering the first auto body panel press for mass production in 1924. Being closely related to the automotive industry, Schuler introduced large panel transfer systems (1983) and crossbar transfer systems (1990) that mainly attributed to the growing success of the company. In 1999, Schuler became publicly listed and until 2007 has developed into a leading player for forming technology delivering production equipment, tools and dies, process know-how, and services for the entire metalworking industry. Besides press technology, Schuler is world market leader in the field of coin minting. Its leading position is primarily attributed to its system competence (the ability to deliver complete press plants turnkey solutions) and its technological know-how.

At the time of the takeover of MW, Schuler was considered a leading global manufacturer of industrial presses with revenues of approximately EUR 563.4m and more than 3,600 employees.[32] More than 70 percent of revenues were realized abroad reflecting the global character of the business. Approximately 75 percent of revenues are related to OEMs and automotive suppliers that primarily use Schuler's products to manufacture car body components. Therefore, the difficult economic situation for automotive manufacturers coping with high overcapacities and cost pressures contributed to a large part to Schuler's negative EBIT of EUR -1.1m and earnings of EUR -9.5m in 05/06. Also order intakes decreased by -5.8 percent to EUR 515.7m

[32] Financial year end: September 2006.

(Schuler AG 2006). High competition especially in the field of press plant manufacturing (large presses) resulted in losses, as many order intakes had to be accepted below manufacturing costs for strategic reasons and/or to guarantee a minimum utilization of manufacturing capacities.

To cope with those challenges, Schuler launched an internal restructuring program SPEED in May 2006 with expected annual savings of more than EUR 30m. SPEED also focused on a strategic orientation towards automotive suppliers offering more specific products especially in the direction of cost-effective standard modules. Additionally, high-margin business segments such as service and the non-automotive sector were put into focus. In March 2007, Schuler acquired its major competitor MW to secure its position as market leader in the metal forming industry.

Mueller Weingarten

Founded in 1866, Weingarten originally focused on the production of embroidery machines, but quickly switched into the field of metal forming in 1872. Similar to its direct rival Schuler, Weingarten grew primarily through innovations for the automotive industry. In 1925, it introduced the first large mechanical press for the automotive industry. Mueller Weingarten (MW) emerged from a merger between "Maschinenfabrik Weingarten" and "Mueller Pressen- und Maschinen" in 1981 forming a company with around 2,500 employees. MW held a position as strong technological innovator, e.g. through construction of the largest transfer press to date with a total tonnage of 95,000kN in 1998. In 1999, MW acquired Beutler Nova, a Swiss press manufacturer, and Beche & Grohs, a German forging machinery manufacturer, expanding its position in the European press market. With the acquisition of the German Umformtechnik Erfurt in 2001, MW became one of the world leading companies in the metal forming industry active in the business areas of mechanical presses, hydraulic presses, die-casting, massive forming, compact presses, service, tool design, and construction.

At the time of the takeover, MW had to suffer from severe decreases in revenue of -16.4 percent to EUR 336.6m in 2006 (from EUR 403.3m in 2005). This decline was attributed to the weak performance in the business area of mechanical presses. Especially large press plant manufacturing experienced losses through high price competition and reluctant investment behavior of OEMs and automotive suppliers. Top-line development was also reflected in bottom-line results with MW realizing losses of EUR -13.8m in 2006. But as the crisis was not only related to difficult market conditions, the management decided to launch a restructuring program called "MW transformation" along four dimensions: operative excellence, growth, portfolio management, and financial structures. The program included the reduction of headcount, a reduction of overtime, a strict application of flextime instruments, as well as other overhead savings (Mueller Weingarten 2006). The restructuring program targeted to achieve annual effects of more than EUR 11m per year.

4.3.2 Discussion of merger motives and transaction synergies

The primary objective of this study is to evaluate the role and nature of market power rents in the takeover of MW by Schuler. To do so, it is essential to understand the underlying rationale and synergy composition behind the takeover. In the following, we highlight the most important motives which we derive from different information sources that allow for evaluating the transaction from different perspectives. We follow the approach of Graebner and Eisenhardt (2004) and rely on interviews with management board, outside experts, publicly available data (e.g. company statements, press review), and internal information to gain background information about the M&A transaction and the specific role of synergies and market power rents. Along this information we categorize the strategic merger rationale along four dimensions:

Forming a global market leader with high innovation capacities: In a highly competitive market environment the merger allowed Schuler to expand its position as market leader and to increase its market share in the field of forming technology for the metalworking industry to approximately 35 percent globally. The merger positioned Schuler as strong technological leader with high innovation capabilities leading to a clear differentiation from competition. The significantly larger engineering staff provided an opportunity to enter new courses in the development of innovative products ensuring a competitive edge in terms of product portfolio and technological leadership in the market. The R&D spending of approximately seven percent of revenues per year and approximately 15 percent of total employees involved underlines the importance of innovation in this sector (Datamonitor 2008). Furthermore, the financial distress of MW positioned the company as an attractive takeover target in the market. If MW's technological know-how and engineering capability had been acquired by competitors, the new entity would have been a severe threat for Schuler. Therefore, the takeover also constituted an important step for Schuler to secure its leading position and to prevent knowledge drain to competitors.

Complementary product portfolios: Besides the strong competition between Schuler and MW, product portfolios of both firms were rather complementary with only approximately 25-30 percent overlap, mainly in the area of large mechanical presses and larger hydraulic metal sheet presses (Industrieanzeiger 2008). As a result, Schuler's management board decided to sustain the existing product portfolio of both firms[33] in order to secure available know-how and start optimization on component level. In a second step, know-how and joint development products helped to bundle the "best of both companies" allowing Schuler to position itself as a full-line provider in all relevant business segments. Especially in the service segment, both companies complemented each other well in distribution and service structure. For example, while service business of Schuler in Mexico was traditionally weak, MW had a strong presence in this market. In this high-margin segment, the merger allowed to expand service offerings around the globe enabling better customer service and a broader service spectrum.

[33] The exception is the sale of the die-casting business, however, this non-core segment was at disposal already before the merger.

Global presence and access to growth markets: The merger increased Schuler's traditional strong market position in Europe and US and leveraged its global presence and market coverage in terms of distribution and service. Both companies were now able to improve access to important growth markets in Asia and Eastern Europe. For example, both companies were present in China, the market with the strongest expected growth in forthcoming years. The joint presence in the market allowed to set up a joint production cooperation with welding und machining of large parts in Shanghai und assembling in Dalian. This enabled the new Schuler to cope with the trend of local sourcing using local production capacities allowing it to offer OEMs and automotive suppliers a full product portfolio.

Synergies: Apart from strategic motives, the merger was aiming to achieve combined annual synergies of approximately EUR 35m per year. In fact, targeted earnings improvements persisted primarily in effects of better order selection and pricing strategies (market power synergies). Before the merger, during strong competition between Schuler and MW it was common practice that press orders were accepted with negative pre-calculation earnings in order to secure market shares, develop new customers, enter new markets, and/or guarantee capacity utilization. As management interviews confirmed, it happened quite often that Schuler and MW were left as remaining bidders in pitches for large press orders. Due to their technological know-how and quality of presses, they were often able to outperform other competitors. As technology and quality leader, the newly created entity had the positioning in the market to avoid this ruinous pricing competition. As CEO Tonn stated *"through the merger with MW the product prices increased, before the merger they were ruinous, partly even below production costs"* (Reuters 2009). Following the merger, Schuler was able to reduce existing strong price competition by winning customers through non-price parameters (e.g. technological differentiation, global presence, and service offerings). This allowed Schuler to realize a major part of the targeted synergy potentials through market power and corresponding pricing effects. The transaction also included synergy effects out of operational excellence (cost reduction), e.g. through bundling of overhead functions and reduction of administrative costs. Nonetheless, the previously launched restructuring programs "SPEED" and "Transformation MW" limited room for additional cost synergies and the management decided to keep layoffs at a low level to maintain the know-how of the employees within the company. Additional synergies yielded improvements such as product and know-how transfer, joint implementing and development strategies, and methodological process transfer.

Summarizing, the merger allowed Schuler to yield significant synergy gains in form of market power synergies (pricing effects) by diminishing the existing price competition (effect of non-price variables) in the market. Through its positioning as innovation leader, Schuler was able to offer unique technology and product quality to its industry partners allowing for an increase in product prices and a stabilization of the competitive pricing situation.

4.3.3 Description of the acquisition event

On March 27, 2007, Schuler announced that it had acquired in a packaged deal 64.49 percent of MW from Metzler Beteiligungsgesellschaft submitting a mandatory offer to the remaining shareholders at the minimum price described by law. At first, the acquisition was not welcomed by the target company, as years of strong competition in a close regional setting (both headquarters are situated in southern Germany) made it difficult to quickly overcome cultural barriers. Rolf Zimmerman (CEO of MW) conceded that the takeover was not the favored solution as *"we originally planned a stand-alone solution and therefore launched a restructuring program that is well ahead. Nonetheless, the merger makes from a strategic and economic perspective sense, as positive arguments overweigh"* (Stuttgarter Zeitung 2007). Furthermore, he stated that *"the management board of a listed company normally has no influence on a change in ownership nor can it prevent such a transaction. Nevertheless, it must take care that its actions are not to the detriment of the company, its shareholders, and employees"* (Mueller Weingarten 2006).

However, after six years during which MW was perceived as a potential takeover target, the merger brought a stabilization of business (FTD 2007). Those six years began with a first takeover attempt of Schuler in 2001 that was challenged by antitrust authorities claiming a market dominating positioning of the merging companies in the area of large presses. In 2007, due to the changing market environment and the downturn of large press demand by OEMs the antitrust authorities approved the transaction without further constraints. Following its mandatory offer, Schuler acquired 96.5 percent of the outstanding shares until May 15, 2007, and began with a squeeze-out procedure for the remaining shareholders. As Boersen-Zeitung (2007) reported, this process had been finalized in September 2007 including the rejection of shareholder complaints against the squeeze-out. Schuler began filing its application to withdraw MW from quotation and stock market trading. The legal takeover of MW was completed on September 21, 2007 (Foundry Management & Technology 2007), closing the so far largest global takeover in the industry for metal forming.

4.3.4 Specification of the integration process

Empirical research highlights repeatedly the importance of the post-merger integration phase (e.g. Gates and Very 2003; Weber and Camerer 2003). Following Ficery, Herd, and Pursche (2007), only 45 percent of the senior executives polled in a 2006 Accenture/Economist Intelligence Unit survey affirmed that expected (cost) synergies had been captured. Aware of this fact, management of Schuler took immediate actions to enable the successful operational and cultural integration of the two firms.

In a first approach, working groups staffed with experts from both companies were set up along the strategic product groups to promote immediate cooperation among both companies, know-how exchange, and realization of synergies. Every working group was directly supervised by a member of the Schuler management board to highlight the priority of the integration work for the future firm. An integration schedule provided clear targets including the assessment of product overlaps, a comparison of segment organization, a joint sales and distribution plan for the following years, and an estimation about the synergy potential in the respective area. The results of the working groups provided a new operational and organizational structure for Schuler. Most of MW operations were integrated directly whereas large and standard press segments were, on short-term, maintained as individual business units.

Figure 4.1 New organizational structure Schuler

This figure illustrates the new organizational structure of Schuler after the integration of the MW divisions. The new organization was build based on the provided new segment organization of the respective working groups.

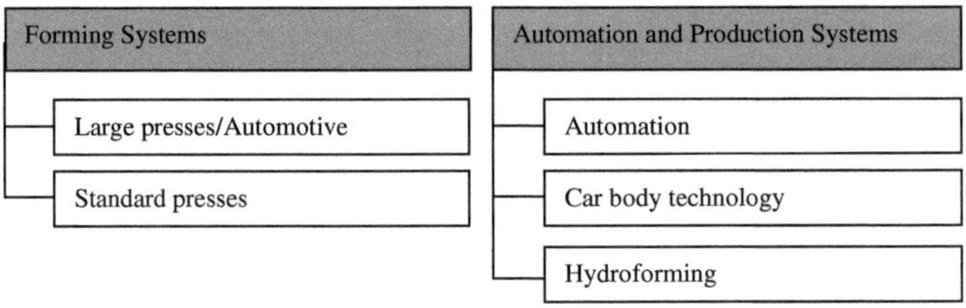

The former competitors invested much effort to quickly overcome cultural barriers and grow into a joint company. While cooperation of Schuler and MW employees seemed to flourish on working level, the management level of MW was replaced by Schuler. At the beginning of July 1, 2007, Schuler's management board member Dr. Beyer took over the CEO position at MW, replacing former CEO Zimmermann. In addition, Schuler board member Dr. Ernst took over management responsibility at MW. Already one year after the transaction, Schuler management board announced that most of the integration targets were achieved. In October 2008, CEO Tonn stated *"the integration process of MW is almost finished"* (Maschinenmarkt

2008). This development was also reflected in regular synergy reports that were established to track the implementation and realization of the identified synergies. The post-merger integration process was a success in quickly realizing the pre-established targets of the integration. A close cooperation from the beginning of the transaction made it possible to realize both, market power potentials and internal efficiency improvements. In the following section we examine whether the internally perceived success of pre- and post-merger integration is also reflected in external capital market reactions and accounting figures.

4.4 Acquisition performance

4.4.1 The capital market perspective

To understand external evaluation and market perception of the Schuler and MW merger, we follow methodology of preceding case study research[34] and analyze share price information applying a combination of different event study methodologies including the standard market model over short-term event windows and the buy and hold abnormal return method over a long-term period (Kaplan, Mitchell, and Wruck 1997). We measure short-term announcement returns by applying the standard market model as described by Brown and Warner (1985) calculating abnormal returns by the difference between expected return (estimated by the market model) and actual returns observed in the market. Abnormal returns for firm i at date t (AR_{it}) are estimated as $AR_{it} = R_{it} - \alpha_i - \beta_i R_{mt}$, where R_{mt} represents the return of the Datastream world industrial machinery index. Market model parameters are estimated over an observation period of 250 trading days starting at day T_{-300} to T_{-50} relative to the announcement date T_0 (March 27, 2007). Market models are estimated performing an ordinary leased squared (OLS) regression over various event windows ranging between two days[-1;+1] and forty days [-20;+20].

Comparing share price developments of Schuler and MW in 2007 (figure 4.2), the direct effect of the merger announcement can be observed. Upon merger announcement, the share price of MW shows the typical strong increase of target firms following a takeover offer. It increases by almost 20 percent from EUR 16.40 to EUR 19.75 at the announcement date. Against typical bidder reactions, also the share price of Schuler increases by 8.5 percent to EUR 6.40 on the same day. We interpret this market reaction as an expression of the strategic rationale and possible synergies associated with the merger. In the days following the merger announcement, the share

---

[34] Other case studies exploring the value creation through M&A include e.g. the takeover of Cameron Iron Works by Cooper Industries and of Florida Tile by Penmark (Kaplan et al. 1997), the merger of Exxon-Mobil (Weston 2002), and the takeover of Conoco by Dupont (Ruback 1982).

of Mueller Weingarten decreases to a more moderate level, in line with the proceeding of offering the minimum price described by law to the remaining shareholders. Meanwhile, Schuler's share experiences further strong growth in May 2007 when it announces that it has acquired 96.47 percent of MW allowing to start with the squeeze-out procedure to gain full control (Stuttgarter Zeitung 2007).

Figure 4.2 Share price development Schuler and MW 2007

This figure illustrates the share price development of the Schuler and MW share for the year 2007. The announcement date of the takeover is on March 27, 2007.

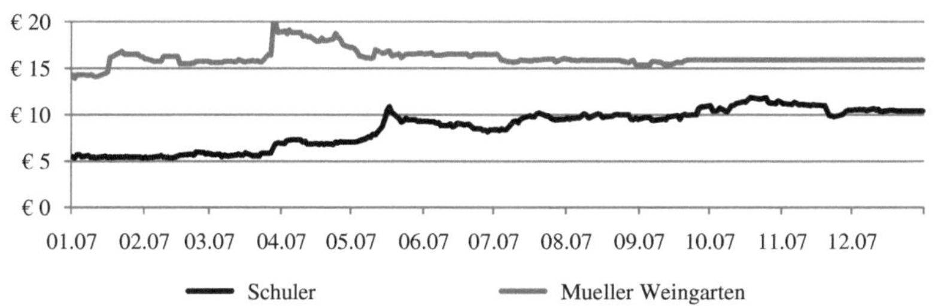

Short-term abnormal return analysis confirms the first positive evaluation of the merger (table 4.1). Both companies show highly positive abnormal returns around the announcement date suggesting an improved market positioning and positive future expectations for the combined entity. While the reaction of MW share with a cumulated abnormal return of around 20 percent is within the typical development for target companies, the strong abnormal return of Schuler with approximately 20 percent is extraordinary high. As Geiger, Schiereck, and Wald (2009) show for mergers and acquisitions in the machinery industry bidders usually react positively, but on a lower average abnormal return of 1.67 percent for the [-1;+1] event window. This finding is in contrast to other cross-sectional research which concludes that abnormal returns to acquirers are potentially zero (Mulherin and Boone 2000; Brunner 2002) or negative

(Walker 2000; DeLong 2001; Houston, James, and Ryngaert 2001; Benoua and Madura 2005). The positive capital market reaction of the Schuler stock can therefore be interpreted as a signal for a favorable merger evaluation that highlights strategic and operational synergies.

To measure the impact of the transaction on the industry environment, abnormal returns of key competitors are analyzed (table 4.1). We concentrate on publicly listed companies that are matched into two different peer sets according to relatedness of businesses. Peer group I compromises direct, single-business, metal forming competitors Amada Co., Hitachi Zosen Fukui Corporation and Aida Engineering. In peer group II, multi-business, metal forming manufacturers with a wider range of operations are included. Peer group II includes the companies Komatsu Ltd., Andritz, IHI Corporation and Kawasaki Heavy Industries. Analyzing market reactions of competitors, negative announcement returns occur across all peer groups. As expected, impact on competitor peer group I is stronger than on competitor peer group II, as the multi-business diversification in peer group II dilutes overall business impact. The major part of negative abnormal returns for rival firms does not cumulate at the day of the merger announcement, but in the 20 days following the merger. We relate this delayed interpretation of merger impact to a waiting attitude of rival investors towards the acceptance of the takeover bid by MW shareholders. The negative rival reactions are against most empirical evidence that primarily documents positive abnormal returns of rival companies around the announcement date (Eckbo (1983), Schumann (1993), Song and Walkling (2000), Fee and Thomas (2004)). According to Eckbo and Wier (1985), negative rival returns can be explained both with the market power theory and the productive efficiency theory if either the acquisition results in predatory conduct or in competitive advantages for the merged firm.

Table 4.1 Short-term abnormal returns of MW, Schuler, and rival companies

This table shows cumulative abnormal returns (CAR) to MW, Schuler, and two groups of competitors (peer group I and peer group II) around the announcement date on March 27, 2007. Competitor peer group I includes publicly listed direct competitors Amada, Hitachi, and Aida.[35] Peer group II includes direct competitors Komatsu, Andritz, IHI, and Kawasaki with broader business portfolios not limited to manufacturing of metal forming machinery.

Event window	MW	Schuler	Competitor (peer I)	Competitor (peer II)	Competitors (all)
[-20;+20]	0.19%	0.23%	-0.15%	-0.11%	-0.13%
[-10;+10]	0.18%	0.24%	-0.12%	-0.06%	-0.08%
[-5;+5]	0.21%	0.27%	-0.05%	-0.05%	-0.05%
[-1;+1]	0.21%	0.17%	-0.02%	-0.01%	-0.01%
[0]	0.21%	0.09%	-0.01%	0.00%	0.00%
[0;+1]	0.21%	0.16%	0.00%	-0.02%	-0.01%
[0;+5]	0.17%	0.22%	-0.02%	-0.04%	-0.04%
[0;+10]	0.14%	0.20%	-0.04%	-0.05%	-0.04%
[0;+20]	0.15%	0.20%	-0.09%	-0.10%	-0.10%

To analyze the long-term impact of the merger, figure 4.3 shows the long-term share price development of the Schuler stock against two selected machinery indices, the Datastream world machinery index and the Datastream Germany industrial engineering index. Following the merger on March 27, 2007, Schuler outperforms the indices reaching its peak during the years 2007 and 2008. However, with the beginning of the crisis within the automotive industry, Schuler shares decrease to a price level similar to comparable indices. On short-term, the merger effect is highly reflected in the positive share price development, but is later overruled by economic prospects lowering expectations for the performance of Schuler and the entire industry. Nonetheless, this finding contradicts more recent event studies on long-term performance that observe negative returns to acquirer shareholders (André, Kooli, and L'Her 2004; Gregory and Matatko 2004).

[35] Peer group I does not include direct competitor Hitachi Zosen Fukui as not sufficient trading days are available.

Figure 4.3 Long-term share price development Schuler and indices

This figure illustrates the share price development of Schuler and its indices from January 2007 until July 2009. As indices serve the Datastream world machinery index and the Datastream Germany industrial engineering index.

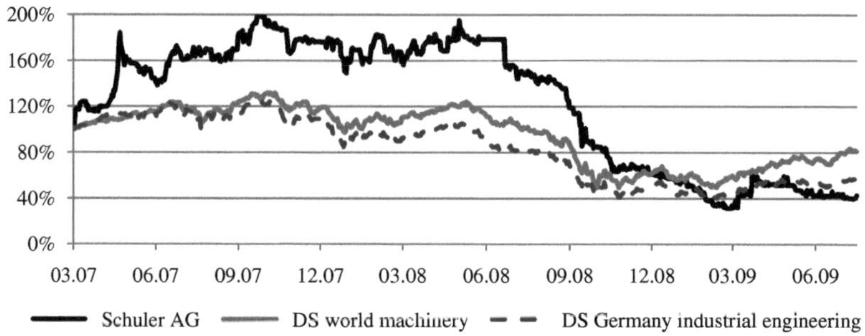

In order to better understand abnormal return behavior, Schuler's return development is challenged against its competitor peer-groups described above. We measure long-term buy and hold abnormal returns (BHARs), where a fictive investment date of 50 days before the merger announcement date is measured against several exit dates in the future (T_{-50}). Schuler's abnormal returns are derived as the difference between the buy and hold return of an investor in Schuler and the buy and hold return of an investor in an equally-weighted portfolio of control firms (Datastream machinery index, peer group I and II). The results are shown in table 4.2.

Table 4.2 Long-term abnormal returns to Schuler – different approaches

This table shows the abnormal buy and hold returns (BAHR) to Schuler against a different set of competitors (peer group I and peer group II) around the announcement date on March 27, 2007. BAHR index constitutes the Datastream machinery index.

Approach	6 months	12 months	18 months	24 months
BAHR index	56.8%	73.3%	59.8%	-4.5%
BAHR peer group I	89.5%	103.5%	106.8%	18.4%
BAHR peer group II	69.4%	106.8%	89.0%	13.9%
BAHR all peers	78.0%	105.4%	96.6%	15.8%

Over a six month holding period an investor in Schuler yields positive abnormal returns between 57 percent and 89 percent compared to an equivalent investment in index or peers. The results confirm the finding of previous short-term analysis indicating an over-performance against competitors. This gap is even larger comparing abnormal returns for the 12 months and 18 months period, when return developments of Schuler shares are twice as high as comparable investments in peer companies. As recent empirical evidence summarizes, the finding of strong positive BAHR effect contrasts normal long-term developments after mergers. For example, Pautler (2003) provides a summary of business consulting literature documenting that less than half of the analyzed mergers succeed in long-term value creation. Rau and Vermaelen (1998) report total negative abnormal returns of -4.0 percent for a three-year period. Comparing the 24 months BAHR of Schuler the pattern changes. Though BAHR, with the exception of index returns, is still positive (ranging from 14 percent to 18 percent) the strong positive development is adjusted to comparable levels. Influenced by the economic downturn, Schuler's strong performance is obviously reduced. A possible explanation for this is provided by Schuler's management arguing that the debt financed takeover of MW results in an additional burden in the crisis increasing the risk of financial leverage.

4.4.2 *The operational performance analysis*

4.4.2.1 Analysis of order income

Published accounting information is used to examine the merger between Schuler and MW with a more detailed view on realized synergies and the impact of economic developments. With its inherent focus on the past, it is not exposed to the subjective assessment of investors who incorporate future expectations into the stock price. Following international accounting standards, Schuler reports its financial statements applying the percentage-of-completion (PoC) method. However, depending on product type, completion of one order can take up to three years (especially in the segment large press manufacturing). Consequently, accounting figures reflect to a large part order backlog of past quarters. To balance this effect, we first analyze the amount and quality of order income that is not prone to this error. Table 4.3 provides an overview of order income development of Schuler on a quarterly basis. Q2 07 is the first quarter including consolidated information of the merged companies.

In the three quarters following the merger, order income of Schuler is exceptionally high increasing from EUR 203.5m in Q2 07 to EUR 410.2m in Q4 07. The typical cyclicality of Schuler's business becomes evident, when comparing the first quarter order income levels across years. Lower order income levels in Q1 09 and Q2 09 reflect negative developments because of the economic crisis. To examine whether the increased order income originates from the takeover or general market conditions, we observe the relative order income growth compared to rival companies. Confirming initial interpretations, Schuler is able to realize significant abnormal order income growth especially in Q3 07 and Q4 07 with 79 percent and 58 percent abnormal performance, respectively. Lower figures in Q1 08 and Q2 09 are below rival levels, but may reflect the normal business cyclicality of Schuler. Interviews with Schuler management not only confirm the above average order development, but also highlight the simultaneous improvement of order profitability and pricing levels.

Furthermore, results indicate that Schuler outperforms its rival companies also during the recent economic crisis reflected in the above average order income between Q4 08 and Q2 09.

Table 4.3 Overview absolute and relative quarterly order income Schuler

This table shows the quarterly order income development of Schuler AG following the merger. Q2 07 is the first quarter reporting consolidated figures. Abnormal order income development is measured against Schuler peer competitors based on the reference quarter Q2 07.

	Q2 07	Q3 07	Q4 07	Q1 08	Q2 08	Q3 08	Q4 08	Q1 09	Q2 09
Order Income (million)	203.5	361.5	410.2	145.3	222.7	228.0	183.5	113.0	146.5
Order Income Growth (Q2 07)	-	78.5%	102.6%	-28.2%	10.0%	12.6%	-9.4%	-44.2%	-27.7%
Relative Order Income Growth	-	79.1%	57.8%	-57.7%	3.0%	10.0%	33.7%	-28.7%	24.9%

4.4.2.2 Financial statement analysis

Besides quarterly order income information, Schuler reports its financial statements on a semi-annually basis with a first consolidation of MW figures during the second half of its fiscal year end September 06/07. Accounting performance until first half of Schuler's fiscal year 08/09 (ended March 2009) is analyzed to gain a thorough understanding of merger impact and accounting figure development. Table 4.4 shows the development of profit and loss as well as balance sheet structure of Schuler.

The first consolidation of MW takes place in the second half of Schuler fiscal year 06/07 and is reflected in corresponding assets and sales growth. The debt increase in the second half of 06/07 indicates the primarily debt-financed purchase of MW. While initial profit data reflects integration costs and the difficult economic situation of MW, accounting figures illustrate a successive improvement of profitability in fiscal year 07/08. Analyzing the development of employees and personnel costs it becomes evident that there are no significant cost synergies realized, as figures remain relatively stable across the observation period. In first half of year 07/08 an improvement in the debt/equity ratio can be observed. However, this is attributed to a sale-and-rent-back transaction of Schuler, where cash-flows are used to reduce outstanding debts. The first half of year 08/09 reflects the impact of economic crisis showing decreasing profits through low operating performance (operating cash flow). Nonetheless, a high order backlog from recent years allows to sustain sales levels and to keep utilization rates high. To cope with new challenges of the market environment, Schuler launches a restructuring program in the last observation period, noticeable in reduced Capex and employee figures.

Table 4.4 Key profit & loss and balance sheet data of Schuler

Schuler fiscal year is from October-September. Profit figures (EBITDA, EBIT, EBT, Net Income, and Operating Cash-flow) in second half of 06/07 are adjusted for one-time effects of a sale-and-rent-back transaction of EUR 30.1m.

Schuler *Fiscal year [EUR m]*	03/31/07 *1. half 06/07*	09/30/07 *2. half 06/07*	03/31/08 *1. half 07/08*	09/30/08 *2. half 07/08*	03/31/09 *1. half 08/09*
Key profit & loss data					
Sales	239.5	485.5	418.3	547.8	442.4
EBITDA	15.6	28.2	31.1	33.6	26.6
EBIT	7.7	7.6	16.6	20.1	12.7
Net Income	4.2	-20.9	4.1	4.5	-1.1
Key balance sheet data					
Total assets	533.7	852.4	866.7	866.7	801.4
Debt	433.3	704.1	687.2	687.2	624.1
Equity	100.4	148.3	179.5	179.5	177.3
Other performance data					
Operating cash-flow	-11.7	-12.0	0.0	-17.1	-38.1
Order backlog	360.5	699.6	836.8	739.7	593.8
Employees	3,520	5,710	5,520	5,634	5,466
Personnel costs	100.2	164.1	161.6	162.0	162.2
Capex	3.1	13.3	13.9	9.1	6.0

This development pattern is also reflected in the analysis of absolute and relative profit oriented, revenue oriented, and balance-sheet oriented performance indicators illustrated in table 4.5: The performance figures reflect the cyclicality of Schuler's business with a better performance in the second half of the year (e.g. revenue oriented performance indicators). At first sight, the merger leads to a decrease in key accounting performance (second half of 06/07) attributed to the consolidation of MW, integration costs, and delayed integration effects that are usually realized on a longer timeframe (panel A table 4.5). However, the positive merger effect can be observed at the beginning of first half 07/08 with profit oriented figures above or similar to Schuler's level before the transaction and followed by a continuous improvement of balance-sheet performance. We interpret this as signal for the successful extortion of market power synergies. In the last reporting period (first half of 08/09), the impact of the economic downturn can primarily be observed in negative operating cash-flows as well as decreasing profitability indicators.

To adjust for the impact of general market conditions, the performance indicators of peer companies are subtracted from Schuler's to analyze the relative performance against competition (panel B table 4.5). A difficult performance situation of Schuler becomes evident, as in basically all major indicators Schuler performs below the average of its competitors prior to the merger. Especially operating cash-flow and efficiency ratios (e.g. sales/employees) indicate major disadvantages of Schuler against competition. The integration of MW further decreases relative performance levels in second half of 06/07. However, the with realization of integration synergies a subsequent improvement of performance can be observed (reduction of underperformance) confirming the positive capital market evaluation. The positive development path reflects the merger synergies that seem primarily attributed to market power rents.

Table 4.5 Selected performance indicators of Schuler

Schuler fiscal year is from October-September. Profit figures (EBITDA, EBIT, EBT, Net Income, and Operating Cash-flow) in second half of 06/07 are adjusted for one-time effects of a sale-and-rent-back transaction of EUR 30.1m.

Schuler *Fiscal year*	03/31/07 *1. half 06/07*	09/30/07 *2. half 06/07*	03/31/08 *1. half 07/08*	09/30/08 *2. half 07/08*	03/31/09 *1. half 08/09*
Panel A: Schuler performance indicators					
Profit oriented performance indicators					
EBITDA/sales	6.5%	5.8%	7.4%	6.1%	6.0%
EBIT/sales	3.2%	1.6%	4.0%	3.7%	2.9%
Operating CF/sales	-4.9%	-2.5%	0.0%	-3.1%	-8.6%
Revenue oriented performance indicators					
Sales/total assets	44.9%	57.0%	48.3%	63.2%	55.2%
Sales/Empl. (TEUR)	68.0	85.0	75.8	97.2	80.9
Balance-sheet structure (in %)					
Equity/total assets	18.8%	17.4%	20.7%	20.7%	22.1%
Debt/equity-ratio	431.8%	474.8%	382.8%	382.8%	352.0%
Panel B: relative Schuler performance indicators					
Profit oriented performance indicators					
EBITDA/sales	-0.9%	-5.6%	-3.6%	-1.8%	0.0%
EBIT/sales	-5.1%	-5.8%	-4.7%	-3.1%	0.8%
Operating CF/sales	-21.1%	-6.6%	-11.3%	-26.7%	-25.9%
Revenue oriented performance indicators					
Sales/total assets	14.5%	34.3%	21.9%	40.6%	31.9%
Sales/empl. (TEUR)	-99.1	-64.1	-96.3	-56.7	-91.1
Balance-sheet structure (in %)					
Equity/total assets	-22.0%	-24.1%	-21.2%	-21.1%	-20.9%
Debt/equity-ratio	183.5%	227.4%	137.8%	140.0%	91.9%

4.5 Summary and conclusion

In this paper we explore the role of market power rents in the value creation process in mergers and their role in shaping the competitive landscape. Overcoming methodological shortcomings of broader empirical studies, we use a case study to examine the takeover of MW by Schuler on March 27, 2007, a transaction that was to a large part motivated by market power rents. Highlighting the background and motives of the transaction, we examine short- and long-term capital market performance as well as post-merger accounting performance of target, acquirer, and rival firms to gain a thorough understanding of implied industry changes.

The analyzed transaction represents a major change in the metal forming industry creating the market leader with approximately 35 percent market share in large mechanical and hydraulic presses (Metalworking Insiders' Report 2007). The merger further expands Schuler's technological leadership in competition leading to a dominance in high-quality presses. This allows Schuler to realize significant market power rents, primarily through the stabilization of pricing levels in the industry. This characteristic is reflected in highly positive capital market evaluation around the announcement date. While target's shareholders are able to realize abnormal wealth gains of 18 percent in an event window of ten days before and ten days after the merger, acquirer shareholders achieve 24 percent positive abnormal share price development. The positive development is also observable in the evaluation of accounting figures of Schuler. Key profitability figures report a successive improvement which is weakened because of effects from the economic crisis at the end of year 2008. Additionally, accounting figures confirm that the transaction was not motivated by major cost synergies, as personnel costs and number of employees remain almost stable across the different reporting periods.

Around the announcement date, competitors react with negative abnormal returns. As the transaction is primarily motivated by market power rents, this reaction seems surprising, as raising product prices should also improve the situation of rival firms (Stigler 1964; Chatterjee 1986; Trautwein 1990; Sharur 2005). In contrast to classic interpretation of capital market reactions, rival companies do not evaluate the positive effects on factor prices as dominant (otherwise they would profit themselves), but rather experience competitive disadvantages e.g. through technological differentiation and/or service coverage. On a long-term perspective, peer companies perform lower than Schuler, as BAHR are highly positive for Schuler (even besides Schuler's over-performance decreases because of the economic crisis). An analysis of abnormal order income shows that rival firms seem not able to profit from increased order income levels. Key performance indicators follow a similar pattern: Though performance levels of Schuler are at first behind the average of its competitors, a positive development path following the merger is observed.

The question remains why Schuler is able to realize such significant synergy gains from the transaction and why this advantage is not available to rival companies. Conducting market analysis and interviews with Schuler management, we conclude that this is possible as product prices are sensitive to changes in non-price competition. Offering non-price factors such as leading technology, a full-line product portfolio, and global service coverage, clients accept increases in product prices. Furthermore, the transaction induces a reduction of existing competition in the high-tech segment of metal forming products that subsequently lead to a general positive price development for Schuler. Even though rival firms are able to partly participate from the increased demand from the automotive industry in 07/08, Schuler profits from its position as market and technology leader. Rival firms that in many cases concentrate on cost-leadership experience negative developments, as they are not able to imitate non-price competition parameters. We conclude that the merger is highly successful in achieving competitive advantages for Schuler through non-price variables allowing Schuler to realize significant market power rents.

Our results suggest that research on merger motive and market power rents should consider impact of non-price variables in merger situations. Especially large scale studies are prone to a distortion of results if relationships and logic among market power mergers and non-price competition are not carefully considered. The suggested explanations can serve as a fruitful basis for further research.

5 Concluding remarks

This doctoral thesis follows the objective of thoroughly examining nature and impact of mergers and acquisitions in the machinery industry. I first evaluate merger motives and benefits in consideration of underlying industry environments. In addition, I examine wealth mechanics and value drivers focusing on the role of corporate relatedness in mergers, before I provide additional insights into merger rent generation on a case study basis. By addressing these questions I aim to close three important empirical research gaps.

First, I examine the influence of industry concentration on merger motives (section 2). Building on theoretical frameworks of industrial organization theory and financial research I argue that exogenous market factors (e.g. industry concentration) should determine endogenous market conduct (industry motives). As a direct parameterization is difficult, I follow recommendation of literature and investigate share price reactions to a new data set of 330 machinery mergers between 1997 and 2007. The results provide additional perspectives on the empirical analysis of research motives behind mergers helping to fill an important research gap. I observe significantly different capital market reactions among merger announcements in dependence of underlying industry concentration. This suggests that different takeover motives prevail in fragmented and concentrated industries. Against existing empirical research (e.g. Trautwein 1990; Fee and Thomas 2004; Ghosh 2004), I find support for monopolistic collusion motives in fragmented industries. Additionally, the analysis provides explanations why broader empirical studies sometimes fail to identify monopolistic motives: First, in concentrated industries monopolistic collusion seems to be successfully impeded by antitrust legislation. Second, in fragmented industries only a limited number of merger transactions is able to realize market power gains. Overall, these findings underline that the general market background should be considered in empirical analysis of merger motives.

After analyzing motives and merger rationale of machinery manufacturers, I thoroughly examine wealth determinants and mechanics in mergers (section 3). Analyzing a data set of 330 machinery mergers, I contribute to the ongoing discussion on corporate focus and diversification. Classifying horizontal, vertical/complementary, and unrelated mergers, I observe that relatedness has significant influence on wealth creation in mergers. In both, univariate and cross-sectional regression, I confirm a positive relationship between acquirer abnormal returns and empirical measures of corporate relatedness. The findings are also robust in the presence of secondary segment information. My results empirically support the positive influence of corporate focus, but also reject the proposition that diversification destroys value, as diversification shows positive average abnormal returns for acquirer and target firms. However, corporate strategies on business focus should account for vertical integration implications, as vertical forward integration shows similar positive wealth effects as horizontal mergers. Results also suggest that the individual characteristics of target and acquirer firm are significant wealth determinants in transactions underlining the management's role in target selection and target integration.

After analyzing empirical findings based on large data samples of machinery transactions, I examine in detail the takeover of Mueller Weingarten by Schuler in March 2007 (section 4). By conducting case study analysis, I am able to illuminate sources and mechanics of merger rents and to provide additional insights into transaction details. I document that the takeover of its major rival enables Schuler to reduce existing fierce price competition in the market and turn competition parameters towards non-price variables resulting in significant merger rents. This is reflected in high capital market gains and accounting data performance. The transaction induces a reduction of existing competition in the high-tech segment of metal forming products that subsequently leads to a general positive product price development for Schuler. Offering non-price factors such as leading technology, a full-line product portfolio, and global service coverage, clients accept an increase in product prices. Rival firms that, in many cases, concentrate on cost-leadership in production experience negative developments as they are not able to imitate non-price competition parameters. Results suggest that research should consider the impact of non-price variables in merger situations. Especially large scale studies are prone to a distortion of results if relationships and logic among market power mergers and non-price competition are not carefully considered.

My analyses confirm that mergers and acquisitions in the machinery industry are particularly suitable to fence against changing market environments and increasing cost pressure from low-cost competitors and globally sourcing customers while operational excellence and innovation in production and development processes of machinery manufacturers is becoming more important. In the presence of positive acquirer and combined entity shareholder returns, I conclude that machinery manufacturers are highly successful in realizing synergies and earning potentials in mergers. The results also imply that takeovers are a powerful way to improve the individual market positioning by shaping the industry environment and gaining competitive advantages against rival firms. I empirically document the wealth determinants and mechanics in machinery mergers highlighting the role of relatedness between target and acquirer. However, results also confirm that the individual position, know-how, and experience of both target and acquirer are major influence factors on wealth generation in mergers. Considering short-term and long-term capital market evaluations, my results confirm that managers can make choices to materially influence the profitability of mergers.

My findings have provided insights reaching beyond implications for the machinery industry. A deeper understanding of vertical integration implications in the discussion on corporate focus should be regarded as another motivation for further research in this area helping firms to choose the appropriate business model and to make the right value chain decisions. The observations on industry influence on merger motives may be an initial point for further research in this area. Further analysis may lead to additional empirical evidence and allows to sharpen conclusions of merger motive research. Both, my theoretical and related empirical evidence provided may serve as orientation for further research in this area.

References

AKHIGBE, AIGBE, STEPHEN F. BORDE and ANN MARIE WHYTE (2000). "The Source of Gains to Targets and Their Industry Rivals: Evidence Based on Terminated Merger Proposals." *Financial Management*, 29(4): 101-118.

ALMAZAN, ANDRES and CARLOS A. MOLINA (2002). "Intra-Industry Capital Structure Dispersion." McCombs Research Paper Series, Austin, *The University of Texas*.

AMIHUD, YAKOV and BARUCH LEV (1981). "Risk Reduction as a Managerial Motive for Conglomerate Mergers." *Bell Journal of Economics*, 12(2): 605-617.

ANDRADE, GREGOR, MARK MITCHELL and ERIK STAFFORD (2001). "New Evidence and Perspectives on Mergers." *The Journal of Economic Perspectives*, 15(2): 103-120.

ANDRADE, GREGOR and ERIK STAFFORD (2004). "Investigating the Economic Role of Mergers " *Journal of Corporate Finance*, 10(1): 1-36.

ANDRÉ, PAUL, MAHER KOOLI and JEAN-FRANCOIS L'HER (2004). "The Long-Run Performance of Mergers and Acquisitions: Evidence from the Canadian Stock Market." *Financial Management*, 33(4): 27-43.

ASQUITH, PAUL, ROBERT F. BRUNER and DAVID W. JR. MULLINS (1983). "The Gains to Bidding Firms from Mergers." *Journal of Financial Economics*, 11(1-4): 121-139.

AZZAM, AZZEDDINE M. (1997). "Measuring Market Power and Cost-Efficiency Effects of Industrial Concentration." *The Journal of Industrial Economics*, 45(4): 377-386.

BAIN, JOE S. (1954). "Economies of Scale, Concentration, and the Condition of Entry in Twenty Manufacturing Industries " *The American Economic Review*, 44(1): 15-39.

BAKER, JONATHAN B. (2003). "The Case for Antitrust Enforcement." *The Journal of Economic Perspectives*, 17(4): 27-50.

BARNEY, JAY B. (1997). "Gaining and Sustaining Competitive Advantage", *Prentice Hall, 2nd Edition*, New Jersey.

BENOUA, GEORGINA and JEFF MADURA (2005). "High-tech Acquisitions, Firm Specific Characteristics, and the Role of Investment Bank Advisors " *The Journal of High Technology Management Research*, 16(1): 101-120.

BERKOVITCH, ELAZAR and M. P. NARAYANAN (1993). "Motives for Takeovers: An Empirical Investigation." *The Journal of Financial and Quantitative Analysis*, 28(3): 247-263.

BOEHMER, EKKEHART, JIM MUSUMECI and ANNETTE B. POULSEN (1991). "Event-Study Methodology under Conditions of Event-Induced Variance." *Journal of Financial Economics*, 30(2): 253-272.

BOERSEN-ZEITUNG (2007). "Schuler secures Entirety of Mueller Weingarten." *Boersen-Zeitung,* September 22, 2007.

BORENSTEIN, SEVERIN and ANDREA SHEPARD (2002). "Sticky Prices, Inventories, and Market Power in Wholesale Gasoline Markets." *The RAND Journal of Economics*, 33(1): 116-139.

BRADLEY, MICHAEL, ANAND DESAI and HAN E. KIM (1988). "Synergistic Gains from Corporate Acquisitions and their Division between the Stockholders of Target and Acquiring Firms." *Journal of Financial Economics*, 21(1): 3-40.

BROWN, STEPHEN J. and JEROLD B. WARNER (1985). "Using Daily Stock Returns: The Case of Event Studies " *Journal of Financial Economics*, 14(1): 3-31.

BRUNNER, ROBERT F. (2002). "Does M&A pay? A Survey for the Decision-maker." *Journal of Applied Finance*, 12(1): 48-60.

BUREAU OF ECONOMIC ANALYSIS (2008). "Industry Economic Accounts", *US Department of Commerce*, Washington.

CAMPA, JOSE MANUEL and SIMI KEDIA (2002). "Explaining the Diversification Discount." *The Journal of Finance*, 57(4): 1731-1762.

CAPRON, LAURENCE (1999). "The Long-Term Performance of Horizontal Acquisitions." *Strategic Management Journal*, 20(11): 987-1018.

CHATTERJEE, SAYAN (1986). "Types of Synergy and Economic Value: The Impact of Acquisitions on Merging and Rival Firms." *Strategic Management Journal*, 7(2): 119-139.

CHATTERJEE, SAYAN, MICHAEL H. LUBATKIN, DAVID M. SCHWEIGER and YAAKOV WEBER (1992). "Cultural Differences and Shareholder Value in Related Mergers: Linking Equity and Human Capital." *Strategic Management Journal*, 13(5): 319-334.

CHATTERJEE, SAYAN (2007). "Why is Synergy so Difficult in Mergers of Related Businesses?" *Strategy & Leadership*, 35(2): 46-52.

CHEN, YONGMIN (2001). "On Vertical Mergers and Their Competitive Effects." *The RAND Journal of Economics*, 32(4): 667-685.

CHURYK, NATALIE T. and RICHARD E. BAKER (2004). "An Examination of Industrial Relatedness, Potential Industrial Synergies, and Merger Premiums in Large Corporate Merger Transactions." *Academy of Accounting and Financial Studies Journal*, 8(1): 111-123.

CLELLAND, IAIN J., THOMAS J. DOUGLAS and DALE A. HENDERSON (2006). "Testing Resource-based and Industry Factors in a Multi-level Model of Competitive Advantage Creation " *The Academy of Management Journal*, 5(1): 1-24.

CME (2004). "Global Trends in Manufacturing", *Canadian Manufacturers and Exporters*, Ottawa.

COASE, RONALD H. (1937). "The Nature of the Firm." *Economica*, 4(16): 386-405.

COHEN, RANDOLPH, CHRISTOPHER POLK and TUOMO VUOLTEENAHO (2003). "The Value Spread." *The Journal of Finance*, 58(2): 609-641.

COMMENT, ROBERT and GREGG A. JARRELL (1995). "Corporate Focus and Stock Returns." *Journal of Financial Economics*, 37(1): 67-87.

CORNETT, MARCIA MILLON, JAMIE JOHN MCNUTT and HASSAN TEHRANIAN (2006). "Performance Changes Around Bank Mergers: Revenue Enhancements versus Cost Reductions." *Journal of Money, Credit, and Banking*, 38(4): 1013-1050.

CROCKER, KEITH J. (1983). "Vertical Integration and the Strategic Use of Private Information." *Bell Journal of Economics*, 14(1): 236-248.

CURRY, BRUCE and KENNETH D. GEORGE (1983). "Industrial Concentration: A Survey." *The Journal of Industrial Economics*, 31(3): 203-255.

DATAMONITOR (2008). "Schuler AG - Business Description." *Datamonitor Company Profiles,* July 02, 2008.

DATAMONITOR (2009). "Global Machinery Market Report", *Datamonitor Industry Profiles (0199-2099)*, New York.

DAVIS, JAMES L., EUGENE F. FAMA and KENNETH R. FRENCH (2000). "Characteristics, Covariances, and Average Returns: 1929 to 1997." *The Journal of Finance*, 55(1): 389-406.

DELOITTE (2003). "Mastering Complexity in Global Manufacturing", *A Deloitte Research Global Manufacturing Study*, London.

DELOITTE (2006). "The Service Revolution in Global Manufacturing Industries", *A Deloitte Research Global Manufacturing Study*, Zurich.

DELONG, GAYLE L. (2001). "Stockholder Gains from Focusing versus Diversifying Bank Mergers." *Journal of Financial Economics*, 59(2): 221-252.

DEMSETZ, HAROLD (1973). "Industry Structure, Market Rivalry, and Public Policy." *Journal of Law and Economics*, 16(1): 1-9.

DENIS, DAVID J., DIANE K. DENIS and ATULYA SARIN (1997). "Agency Problems, Equity Ownership and Corporate Diversification." *The Journal of Finance*, 52(1): 135-160.

DENIS, DAVID J., DIANE K. DENIS and KEVEN YOST (2002). "Global Diversification, Industrial Diversification, and Firm Value." *The Journal of Finance*, 57(5): 1951-1979.

DONG, MING, DAVID A. HIRSHLEIFER, SCOTT A. RICHARDSON and SIEW H. TEOH (2002). "Does Investor Misevaluation Drive the Takeover Market?" Working Paper Series, Columbus, Ohio, *The Ohio State University*.

ECKBO, ESPEN B. (1983). "Horizontal Mergers, Collusion, and Stockholder Wealth." *Journal of Financial Economics*, 11(1-4): 241-273.

ECKBO, ESPEN B. and PEGGY WIER (1985). "Antimerger Policy under the Hart-Scott-Rodino Act: A Reexamination of the Market Power Hypothesis." *Journal of Law and Economics*, 28(1): 119-149.

EISENHARDT, KATHLEEN M. and MELISSA E. GRAEBNER (2007). "Theory Building from Cases: Opportunities and Challenges." *The Academy of Management Journal*, 50(1): 25-32.

FAN, JOSEPH P. H. and LARRY H. P. LANG (2000). "The Measurement of Relatedness: An Application to Corporate Diversification." *Journal of Business*, 73(4): 629-660.

FAN, JOSEPH P. H. and VIDHAN K. GOYAL (2006). "On the Patterns and Wealth Effects of Vertical Mergers." *Journal of Business*, 79(2): 877-902.

FEE, EDWARD C. and SHAWN THOMAS (2004). "Sources of Gains in Horizontal Mergers: Evidence from Customer, Supplier, and Rival Firms." *Journal of Financial Economics*, 74(3): 423-460.

FICERY, KRISTIN, TOM HERD and BILL PURSCHE (2007). "Where has all the Synergy gone? The M&A Puzzle." *Journal of Business Strategy*, 28(5): 20-35.

FINKELSTEIN, SYDNEY and JERAYR HALEBLIAN (2002). "Understanding Acquisition Performance: The Role of Transfer Effects." *Organization Science*, 13(1): 36-47.

FOCARELLI, DARIO and FABIO PANETTA (2003). "Are Mergers Beneficial to Consumers? Evidence from the Market for Bank Deposits." *The American Economic Review*, 93(4): 1152-1172.

FONTENAY, CATHERINE C. and JOSHUA S. GANS (2005). "Vertical Integration in the Presence of Upstream Competition." *The RAND Journal of Economics*, 36(3): 544-572.

FOUNDRY MANAGEMENT & TECHNOLOGY (2007). "Schuler AG completed its legal takeover of Muller Weingarten AG " *Foundry Management & Technology,* September 21, 2008.

FOWLER, KAREN L. and DENNIS R. SCHMIDT (1988). "Tender Offers, Acquisitions, and Subsequent Performance in Manufacturing Firms." *The Academy of Management Journal*, 31(4): 962-974.

FTD (2007). "Schuler übernimmt Mueller Weingarten." *Financial Times Deutschland,* 29. March 2007.

FULLER, KATHLEEN, JEFFREY NETTER and MIKE STEGEMOLLER (2002). "What Do Returns to Acquiring Firms Tell Us? Evidence from Firms that Make Many Acquisitions." *The Journal of Finance*, 57(4): 1763-1793.

GATES, STEPHEN and PHILIPPE VERY (2003). "Measuring Performance During M&A Integration." *Long Range Planning*, 36(2): 167-185.

GEIGER, FLORIAN, DIRK SCHIERECK and ANDREAS WALD (2009). "Corporate Relatedness and Wealth Creation in Machinery Mergers ". Working Paper Series, Oestrich-Winkel, *European Business School.*

GHOSH, ALOKE (2004). "Increasing Market Share as a Rationale for Corporate Acquisitions." *Journal of Business Finance & Accounting*, 31(1-2): 209-247.

GOMES, JOAO and DMITRY LIVDAN (2004). "Optimal Diversification: Reconciling Theory and Evidence." *The Journal of Finance*, 59(2): 507-535.

GRAEBNER, MELISSA E. and KATHLEEN M. EISENHARDT (2004). "The Seller's Side of the Story: Acquisition as Courtship and Governance as Syndicate in Entrepreneurial Firms." *Administrative Science Quarterly*, 49(3): 366-403.

GRAHAM, JOHN R., MICHAEL L. LEMMON and JACK G. WOLF (2002). "Does Corporate Diversification Destroy Value?" *The Journal of Finance*, 52(2): 695-720.

GREGORY, ALAN and JOHN MATATKO (2004). "Biases in Estimating Long Run Abnormal Returns and Conditional Measures of Performance: The Evidence on Takeovers Re-Examined." "Working Paper Series", *University of Exeter.*

GROSSMAN, SANFORD J. and OLIVER D. HART (1986). "The Costs and Benefits of Ownership: A Theory of Vertical and Lateral Integration." *The Journal of Political Economy*, 94(4): 691-719.

HARRINGTON, SCOTT E. and DAVID G. SHRIDER (2007). "All Events Induce Variance: Analyzing Abnormal Returns When Effects Vary across Firms." *The Journal of Financial and Quantitative Analysis*, 42(3): 229-256.

HART, OLIVER and JOHN MOORE (1990). "Property Rights and the Nature of the Firm." *The Journal of Political Economy*, 98(6): 1119-1158.

HAYWARD, MATHEW L. A. (2002). "When Do Firms Learn from Their Acquisition Experience? Evidence from 1990-1995." *Strategic Management Journal*, 23(1): 21-39.

HELWEGE, JEAN, CHRISTO PIRINSKY and RENÉ M. STULZ (2007). "Why Do Firms Become Widely Held? An Analysis of the Dynamics of Corporate Ownership." *The Journal of Finance*, 62(3): 995-1028.

HIRSCHEY, MARK (1985). "Market Structure and Market Value." *Journal of Business*, 58(1): 89-98.

HOU, KEWEI (2003). "Industry Information Diffusion and the Lead-Lag Effect in Stock Returns." Working Paper Series, Columbus, Ohio, *The Ohio State University*.

HOU, KEWEI and DAVID T. ROBINSON (2006). "Industry Concentration and Average Stock Returns." *The Journal of Finance*, 61(4): 1927-1956.

HOUSTON, JOEL F., CHRISTOPHER M. JAMES and MICHAEL D. RYNGAERT (2001). "Where do Merger Gains come from? Bank Mergers from the Perspective of Insiders and Outsiders." *Journal of Financial Economics*, 60(2-3): 285-331.

HYLAND, DAVID C. and DAVID J. DILTZ (2002). "Why Firms Diversify: An Empirical Examination." *Financial Management*, 31(1): 5-35.

INDUSTRIEANZEIGER (2008). "Schuler Chef Jürgen Tonn über Aussichten und Trends in der Umformtechnik." *Industrieanzeiger,* November 10, 2008.

JENSEN, MICHAEL C. and RICHARD S. RUBACK (1983). "The Market for Corporate Control: The Scientific Evidence." *Journal of Financial Economics*, 11(1): 5-50.

KAHLE, KATHLEEN M. and RALPH A. WALKLING (1996). "The Impacts of Industry Classifications on Financial Research." *The Journal of Financial and Quantitative Analysis*, 31(3): 309-335.

KALE, JAYANT R. and HUSAYN SHAHRUR (2007). "Corporate Capital Structure and the Characteristics of Suppliers and Customers." *Journal of Financial Economics*, 83(2): 321-365.

KAPLAN, STEVEN N. and MICHAEL S. WEISENBACH (1992). "The Success of Acquisitions: Evidence from Divestitures " *The Journal of Finance*, 47(1): 107-139.

KAPLAN, STEVEN N., MARK L. MITCHELL and KAREN H. WRUCK (1997). "A Clinical Exploration of Value Creation and Destruction in Acquisitions: Organizational Design, Incentives, and Internal Capital Markets." Working Paper Series, Chicago, *Harvard School of Business*.

KNOTT, ANNE MARIE and POSEN HART (2003). "Does competition increase innovation? New evidence from old industries." Working Paper Series, Wharton, *University of Pennsylvania*.

KUKA (2007). "Annual Report 2007".

LAFONTAINE, FRANCINE and MARGARET SLADE (2007). "Vertical Integration and the Firm Boundaries: The Evidence." *Journal of Economic Literature*, 45(3): 629-685.

LANG, LARRY H. P. and RENÉ M. STULZ (1994). "Tobin's q, Corporate Diversification, and Firm Performance " *The Journal of Political Economy*, 102(6): 1248-1280.

LIEN, LASSE B. and PETER G. KLEIN (2008). "Measuring Inter-Industry Relatedness: SIC Distances versus the Survivor Principle." Working Paper Series, Bergen, *Norwegian School of Economics and Business Administration.*

LINS, KARL and HENRI SERVAES (1999). "International Evidence on the Value of Corporate Diversification." *The Journal of Finance*, 54(6): 2215-2239.

LUBATKIN, MICHAEL (1987). "Merger Strategies and Stockholder Value." *Strategic Management Journal*, 8(1): 39-53.

MACKAY, PETER and GORDON M. PHILLIPS (2005). "How Does Industry Affect Firm Financial Structure?" *The Review of Financial Studies*, 18(4): 1433-1466.

MAKSIMOVIC, VOJISLAV and GORDON M. PHILIPPS (2001). "The Market for Corporate Assets: Who Engages in Mergers and Asset Sales and are there Efficiency Gains?" *The Journal of Finance*, 56(6): 2019-2065.

MALMENDIER, ULRIKE and GEOFFREY A. TATE (2002). "Who makes Acquisitions? CEO Overconfidence and the Market's Reaction." Working Paper Series, Cambridge, Massachusetts, *Harvard Business School.*

MASCHINENMARKT (2008). "Mit dickem Auftragspolster Schuler AG hat den Integrationsprozess mit Müller Weingarten nahezu abgeschlossen." *Maschinenmarkt,* October 24, 2008.

MCKINSEY (2004). "A New Look at Diversification." *McKinsey Quarterly,* February 2004.

METALWORKING INSIDERS' REPORT (2004). "Takeover of Manzoni strengthens Pressbuilder Aida in Europe." *Metalworking Insiders' Report,* November 15, 2004.

METALWORKING INSIDERS' REPORT (2007). "Merger of Muller Weingarten into Schuler will create Forming Leader." *Metalworking Insiders' Report,* April 06, 2007.

MITCHELL, MARK and HAROLD J. MULHERIN (1996). "The Impact of Industry Shocks on Takeover and Restructuring Activity." *Journal of Financial Economics*, 41(2): 193-229.

MOELLER, SARA B., FREDERIK P. SCHLINGEMANN and RENÉ M. STULZ (2004). "Firm Size and the Gains from Acquisitions." *Journal of Financial Economics*, 73(2): 201-228.

MONTGOMERY, CYNTHIA A. (1994). "Corporate Diversification." *The Journal of Economic Perspectives*, 8(3): 163-178.

MOROSINI, PIERO, SCOTT SHANE and HARBIR SINGH (1998). "National Cultural Distance and Cross-Border Acquisition Performance." *Journal of International Business Studies*, 29(1).

MORRISON PAUL, J. CATHERINE (2003). "Cost Economies: A Driving Force for Consolidation and Concentration?" *Southern Economic Journal*, 70(1): 110-127.

MPOYI, RICHARD T. (2003). "A Cross-Industry Analysis of Vertical Integration Strategies: an Exploratory Study." *Journal of Business Administration Online*, 2(1): 1-13.

MUELLER WEINGARTEN (2006). "Annual Report 2006".

MULHERIN, HAROLD J. and AUDRA L. BOONE (2000). "Comparing Acquisitions and Divestitures." *The Journal of Corporate Finance*, 6(2): 117-139.

NEUMARK, DAVID and STEVEN A. SHARPE (1992). "Market Structure and the Nature of Price Rigidity: Evidence from the Market for Consumer Deposits." *The Quarterly Journal of Economics*, 107(2): 657-680.

NOCKE, VOLKER and LUCY WHITE (2007). "Do Vertical Merger facilitate Upstream Collusion?" *The American Economic Review*, 97(4): 1321-1339.

ORDOVER, JANUSZ A., GARTH SALONER and STEVEN C. SALOP (1990). "Equilibrium Vertical Foreclosure." *The American Economic Review*, 80(1): 127-142.

PATELL, JAMES M. (1976). "Corporate Forecasts of Earnings per Share and Stock Price Behavior: Empirical Tests." *Journal of Accounting Research*, 14(2): 246-276.

PAUTLER, PAUL A. (2001). "Evidence on Mergers and Acquisitions." Working Paper 243, Washington, *Federal Trade Commission, Bureau of Economics*.

PAUTLER, PAUL A. (2003). "The Effects of Mergers and Post-Merger Integration: A Review of Business Consulting Literature." Working Paper Series, Washington, *Federal Trade Commission, Bureau of Economics*.

PHILLIPS, MARK (2008). "Desperately Seeking Synergy: an Often Promised, Rarely Delivered Outcome." *The Coastal Business Journal*, 7(1): 21-26.

PORTER, MICHAEL E. (1985). "Competitive Advantage: Creating and Sustaining Superior Performance", *Free Press*, New York.

PORTER, MICHAEL E. (1987). "From Competitive Advantage to Corporate Strategy." *Harvard Business Review*, 65(3): 43-59.

PWC (2008). "Producing value: Global Industrial Manufacturing Mergers and Acquisitions Analysis, 2005-2007", *PriceWaterhouseCoopers*, New York.

RAU, RAGHAVENDRA P. and THEO VERMAELEN (1998). "Glamour, Value and the Post-Acquisition Performance of Acquiring Firms." *Journal of Financial Economics* 49(2): 223-253.

RAVENSCRAFT, DAVID J. and F. M. SCHERER (1987). "Life After Takeover." *The Journal of Industrial Economics*, 36(2): 147-156.

RBSC (2005). "Diversify, but do it the Right Way". B. SCHWENKER, *Roland Berger Strategy Consultants*, Munich.

RBSC and VDMA (2007). "Profitable Growth Strategies for Engineered Products Companies", *Roland Berger Strategy Consultants*, Munich.

RBSC (2008). "Trends and Success Patterns in the Machinery Industry", *Roland Berger Strategy Consultants*, Berlin.

REUTERS (2009). "Auftragsboom bei Schuler geht zu Ende." *Reuters,* January 29, 2009.

ROLL, RICHARD (1986). "The Hubris Hypothesis of Corporate Takeovers." *Journal of Business*, 59(2): 197-216.

RUBACK, RICHARD S. (1982). "The Conoco Takeover and Stockholder Returns." *Sloan Management Review*, 23(13): 13-33.

RUMELT, RICHARD P. (1974). "Strategy, Structure, and Economic Performance", *Harvard Business School Press*, Chicago.

RUMELT, RICHARD P. (1991). "How much does Industry Matter?" *Strategic Management Journal*, 12(3): 167-185.

SALINGER, MICHAEL A. (1988). "Vertical Mergers and Market Foreclosure." *The Quarterly Journal of Economics*, 103(2): 345-356.

SCHMALENSEE, RICHARD (1987). "Inter-Industry Studies of Structure and Performance." Working Paper Series 1874-87, Cambridge, Massachusetts, *Sloan School of Management*.

SCHULER AG (2006). "Annual Report 05/06".

SCHUMANN, LAURENCE (1993). "Patterns of Abnormal Returns and the Competitive Effects of Horizontal Mergers." *Review of Industrial Organization*, 8(6): 679-696.

SCHUMPETER, JOSEPH, Ed. (1912). "The Theory of Economic Development", Cambridge.

SERRA, ANA P. (2004). "Event Study Tests: a brief survey." *Revista Electrónica de Gestao Organizacional*, 2(3): 248-255.

SERVAES, HENRI (1996). "The Value of Diversification During the Conglomerate Merger Wave." *The Journal of Finance*, 51(4): 1201-1225.

SETH, ANJU (1990). "Sources of Value Creation in Acquisitions: An Empirical Investigation." *Strategic Management Journal*, 11(6): 431-446.

SEYHUN, NEJAT H. (1990). "Do Bidder Managers Knowingly Pay Too Much for Target Firms?" *Journal of Business*, 63(4): 1439-1466.

SHAHRUR, HUSAYN (2005). "Industry Structure and Horizontal Takeovers: Analysis of Wealth Effects on Rivals, Suppliers, and Corporate Customers." *Journal of Financial Economics*, 76(1): 61-98.

SHAN, LIWEI and WESLEY W. WILSON (2007). "Concentration, Mergers and Profits - Abnormal Returns and Merger Announcements across Industries." Working Paper Series, Chengdu, China, *IWIF II*.

SHARUR, HUSAYN (2005). "Industry structure and horizontal takeovers: Analysis of wealth effects on rivals, suppliers, and corporate customers." *Journal of Financial Economics*, 76(1): 61-98.

SLADE, MARGARET E. (2004). "Competing Models of Firm Profitability." *International Journal of Industrial Organization*, 22(3): 289-308.

SONG, MOON H. and RALPH A. WALKLING (2000). "Abnormal Returns to Rivals of Acquisition Targets: A Test of the "Acquisition Probablility Hypothesis"." *Journal of Financial Economics*, 55(2): 143-171.

STIGLER, GEORGE J. (1964). "A Theory of Oligopoly." *The Journal of Political Economy*, 72(1): 44-61.

STILLMANN, ROBERT (1983). "Examining Antitrust Policy Towards Horizontal Mergers." *Journal of Financial Economics*, 11(1-4): 225-240.

STUTTGARTER ZEITUNG (2007). "Hersteller von Pressen gehen zusammen." *Stuttgarter Zeitung,* March 29, 2007.

TRAUTWEIN, FRIEDRICH (1990). "Merger Motives and Merger Prescriptions." *Strategic Management Journal*, 11(4): 283-295.

US CENSUS BUREAU (2002). "Economic Census", *U.S. Department of Commerce*, Washington.

US DEPARTMENT OF LABOR (2007). "Industry Guide Machinery Manufacturing." *US Department of Labor*, accessed: August 27, 2008, http://www.bls.gov/oco/cg/cgs052.htm#nature.

VDMA (2008). "Global Production Volume Machinery Industry", *Department of Economics and Statistics*, Frankfurt.

VILLALONGA, BELEN (2004). "Diversification Discount or Premium? New Evidence from the Business Information Tracking Series." *The Journal of Finance*, 59(2): 379-506.

WALKER, MARK M. (2000). "Corporate Takeovers, Strategic Objectives, and Acquiring-Firm Shareholder Wealth." *Financial Management*, 29(1): 53-66.

WALKING, RALPH A. and MICHAEL S. LONG (1984). "Agency Theory, Managerial Welfare, and Takeover Bid Resistance." *The RAND Journal of Economics*, 15(1): 54-68.

WEBER, ROBERTO A. and COLIN F. CAMERER (2003). "Cultural Conflict and Merger Failure: An Experimental Approach." *Management Science*, 49(4): 400-415.

WEISS, LEONARD W. (1974). The Concentration-Profits Relationship and Antitrust. "Industrial Concentration: The New Learning. " *Columbia University Press*, New York.

WEISS, LEONARD W. (1989). "Concentration and price", *MIT Press*, Cambridge, Massachusetts.

WEN, JEAN-FRANCOIS (2001). "Market Power in Grocery Retailing: Assessing the Evidence for Canada." Working Paper, Calgary, Alberta, *Bureau of Competition*.

WESTON, FRED J. (2002). "The Exxon-Mobil Merger: an Archetype." *Journal of Applied Finance*, 12(1): 69-88.

WHITE, HALBERT (1980). "A Heteroskedasticity-Consistent Covariance Matrix Estimator and a Direct Test for Heteroskedasticity." *Econometrica*, 48(4): 817-838.

WILCOX, DIXON H., KUO-CHUNG CHANG and VARUN GROVER (2001). "Valuation of Mergers and Acquisitions in the Telecommunications Industry: a Study on Diversification and Firm Size." *Information & Management*, 38(4): 459-471.

WILLIAMSON, OLIVER E. (1979). "Transaction Cost Economies: The Governance of Contractual Relations." *Journal of Law and Economics*, 22(2): 233-261.

GABLER RESEARCH

„Schriften zum europäischen Management"
Herausgeber: Roland Berger Strategy Consultants –
Academic Network
lieferbare Titel (seit 1.1.2006)

Burkhard Schnorrenberg
Zur Preisbildung von Forwardkontrakten im Strommarkt

Leonid Jasvoin
Integration der Unsicherheitsaspekte in die Schedule-Optimierung

Gerd Sievers
Desinvestition von Unternehmensbeteiligungen in Krisensituationen

Carsten Herbes
Post-Merger-Integration bei europäisch-japanischen Unternehmenszusammenschlüssen

Nicholas Richter
Möglichkeiten und Grenzen des Distressed Debt Investing in Deutschland

Michael Zollenkop
Geschäftsmodellinnovation

Tobias Raffel
Unternehmensberater in der Politikberatung

Holger Buschmann
Erfolgreiches Turnaround-Management

Jonna Barth
Corporate Citizenship aus der Sicht der Landespolitik

Tobias Plate
Personalauswahl in Unternehmensberatungen

Andreas Schreiner
Equity Valuation Using Multiples

Oliver Conze
Kundenloyalität durch Kundenvorteile

Stefan Duderstadt
Wertorientierte Vertriebssteuerung durch ganzheitliches Vertriebscontrolling

Rembert Schulze Wehninck
Public Private Partnerships und Wettbewerb

Gerrit Karalus
Wachstumsstrategien in der Medienbranche

Philipp Wohland
E-Commerce-Geschäftsmodelle im deutschen Tourismusmarkt

(Weitere Titel dieser Reihe finden Sie auf der folgenden Seite.)

MIX
Papier aus verantwortungsvollen Quellen
Paper from responsible sources
FSC® C105338

If you have any concerns about our products,
you can contact us on
ProductSafety@springernature.com

In case Publisher is established outside the EU,
the EU authorized representative is:
Springer Nature Customer Service Center GmbH
Europaplatz 3, 69115 Heidelberg, Germany

Printed by Libri Plureos GmbH
in Hamburg, Germany